M000309498

Critical Decisions:

surviving in today's world

A Bible Study Strategy That Builds Christian Community

SERENDIPITY
HOUSE

LIFE
CONNECTIONS

© Copyright 2001, 2003 Serendipity House

All rights reserved

No part of this work may be reproduced or transmitted in any form or
by any means, electronic or mechanical, including photocopying and recording,
or by any information storage or retrieval system, except as may be expressly
permitted in writing by the publisher. Requests for permission should be addressed
in writing to Serendipity House; 117 10th Avenue, North; Nashville, TN 37234.

ISBN: 1-5749-4091-0

Unless otherwise indicated, all Scripture quotations are from the Holy Bible,
New International Version, copyright © 1973, 1978, 1984
by International Bible Society. Used by permission.

To order additional copies of this resource:
ORDER ONLINE at *www.serendipityhouse.com*;
VISIT the LifeWay Christian Store serving you;
WRITE Serendipity House
117 10th Avenue, North
Nashville, TN 37234
FAX (615) 277-8181
PHONE (800) 525-9563

Printed in the United States of America

117 10th Avenue, North
Nashville, Tennessee 37234

03 04 05 06 07 08 / 10 9 8 7 6 5 4 3

Contents

SESSION 1
Choosing Godly Values　　　　　1 John 2:15–17,24–27　　　8

SESSION 2
Choosing to Stand Firm　　　　　Ephesians 6:10–18　　　20

SESSION 3
Choosing Wisdom in Relationships　　　James 3:13–18　　　32

SESSION 4
Choosing to Delight in God　　　　Psalm 37:3–9　　　44

SESSION 5
Choosing God's Will　　　　　Philippians 2:5–11　　　56

SESSION 6
Choosing God's Forgiveness　　　　Hebrews 12:1–11　　　68

SESSION 7
Choosing God's Authority　　　Genesis 2:15–17;3:1–6　　　80

SESSION 8
Choosing to Study God's Word　　　　James 1:22–25　　　92

SESSION 9
Choosing the Holy Spirit's Guidance　　　John 16:5–16　　　102

SESSION 10
Choosing to Grow in Faith　　　Genesis 45:4–11;50:15–21　　　112

SESSION 11
Choosing Godly Counsel　　　　1 Kings 12:1–14　　　124

SESSION 12
Choosing God's Wisdom　　　　James 1:1–12　　　134

SESSION 13
Choosing God's Priorities　　　　James 4:13–17　　　146

Core Values

Community: The purpose of this curriculum is to build community within the body of believers around Jesus Christ.

Group Process: To build community, the curriculum must be designed to take a group through a step-by-step process of sharing your story with one another.

Interactive Bible Study: To share your "story," the approach to Scripture in the curriculum needs to be open-ended and right-brained—to "level the playing field" and encourage everyone to share.

Developmental Stages: To provide a healthy program in the life cycle of a group, the curriculum needs to offer courses on three levels of commitment:

(1) Beginner Level—low-level entry, high structure, to level the playing field;
(2) Growth Level—deeper Bible study, flexible structure, to encourage group accountability;
(3) Discipleship Level—in-depth Bible study, open structure, to move the group into high gear.

Target Audiences: To build community throughout the culture of the church, the curriculum needs to be flexible, adaptable, and transferable into the structure of the average church.

Mission: To expand the kingdom of God one person at a time by filling the "empty chair." (We add an extra chair to each group session to remind us of our mission.)

Group Covenant

It is important that your group covenant together, agreeing to live out important group values. Once these values are agreed upon, your group will be on its way to experiencing Christian community. It's very important that your group discuss these values—preferably as you begin this study. The first session would be most appropriate. (Check the rules to which each member of your group agrees.)

☐ **Priority:** While you are in this course of study, you give the group meetings priority.

☐ **Participation:** Everyone is encouraged to participate and no one dominates.

☐ **Respect:** Everyone is given the right to his or her own opinion, and all questions are encouraged and respected.

☐ **Confidentiality:** Anything that is said in the meeting is never repeated outside the meeting.

☐ **Life Change:** We will regularly assess our own life-change goals and encourage one another in our pursuit of Christlikeness.

☐ **Empty Chair:** The group stays open to reaching new people at every meeting.

☐ **Care and Support:** Permission is given to call upon each other at any time, especially in times of crisis. The group will provide care for every member.

☐ **Accountability:** We agree to let the members of the group hold us accountable to the commitments we make in whatever loving ways we decide upon.

☐ **Mission:** We will do everything in our power to start a new group.

☐ **Ministry:** The group will encourage one another to volunteer and serve in a ministry and to support missions by giving financially and/or personally serving.

For the Leader

Each group meeting consists of a three-part agenda:

Icebreaker – Fun questions designed to warm the group and build understanding about other group members. These questions prepare the group for meaningful discussion throughout the session.

Bible Study – The heart of each session is the Bible study time. The Life Connections series involves six easy-to-understand segments.

1. **Scripture Reading** – Each Bible study begins with the reading of the focal passage.
2. **About Today's Session** – This section of the Bible Study time is designed to peak the interest of attendees and introduce the theme for the session. In most instances there will be a reminder of what was studied the previous week, a captivating illustration or analogy related to everyday life, and a statement describing what life-changing topic will be given attention.
3. **Identifying with the Story** – During this segment of the Bible Study, subgroups learn more about each other by answering questions that will help them share their story. These questions directly relate to the topic for the day.
4. **Today's Session** – This short teaching time will be led by the Master Teacher. These scripted teachings include a depth of biblical understanding, fascinating illustrations, analogies, statistics, and stories that will spark questions and conviction.
5. **Learning from the Story** – Subgroups will gather to answer a series of questions that anticipate commitment to applying the truths taught.
6. **Life Change Lessons** – The Master Teacher gives practical suggestions that will aid attendees in carrying out the commitments they make.

Caring Time – All study should point us to action. Each session ends with prayer and direction in caring for the needs of group members. Time is also provided to pray for the "empty chair." The empty chair is a visible symbol of the need for each group to lead an unbeliever to a relationship with Jesus Christ.

The cross icon and boxed text represents portions of the student book that have been reprinted in this book.

Every Life Connections group must fill three important roles. Each responsibility is vital to the success of the class.

Teacher – The teacher is the key leader of any Life Connections group. It is the responsibility of the teacher to:

1. enlist facilitators and apprentices.
2. make facilitators and apprentices aware of their roles and be certain these responsibilities are carried out.
3. meet periodically with facilitators to train, encourage, and inspire them.
4. cast vision for and keep the group focused on the goals of the group.
5. guide group members to understand and commit to the group covenant.
6. be sure the group utilizes, fills, and evangelizes through use of the empty chair concept.
7. act as the Master Teacher for the group.
8. keep the group on task throughout each session.

Facilitator – Each subgroup will have a facilitator. It is the responsibility of the facilitators to:

1. lead each individual in their subgroup to participate in Icebreaker activities.
2. involve all members in their subgroup in the Identifying with the Story section of the study.
3. guide those in their subgroup to commit to apply the lessons learned in the Learning from the Story section of the weekly session.
4. with sensitivity and wisdom lead their subgroup to minister to one another during the Caring Time and involve their subgroup in ministry and evangelism.
5. minister to the needs of their subgroup members and lead them to minister to the needs of one another both during and between meetings.

Apprentice – Every subgroup must have an apprentice. When the group consistently has eight or more in attendance, the group should divide into two groups. The apprentice will become the facilitator of the new group and choose an apprentice who will someday be the facilitator of a group. It is the role of the apprentice to:

1. learn from the facilitator of their group.
2. make welcome all new subgroup members.
3. be certain student books and pens or pencils are available for all participants.
4. turn in prayer requests.
5. encourage participation by actively participating themselves.
6. lead the group when the facilitator is unavailable.

For more information and frequently asked questions about Life Connections, visit our Web site at *www.serendipityhouse.com*.

Session

1

Choosing Godly Values

Prepare for the Session

	READINGS	REFLECTIVE QUESTIONS
Monday	1 John 2:15	Is there anything in the world you love more than God?
Tuesday	1 John 2:16	How much of your identity is based on what you do or what you own?
Wednesday	1 John 2:17	What is the advantage to committing your life to following the will of God?
Thursday	1 John 2:24–25	How can you "remain in the Son and in the Father" on a daily basis?
Friday	1 John 2:26–27	When have you been led astray? How can you avoid this in the future?
Saturday	Titus 2:11–14	What "worldly passions" give you the most trouble as you live in this present age?
Sunday	2 Peter 3:10–13	What will be your reward for choosing godly values over the world's values?

notes:

1

OUR GOALS FOR THIS SESSION ARE:

⊌ **In groups of 6–8, gather people in a horseshoe configuration.**

Make sure everyone has a name tag.

Take time to share information on class parties that are coming up as well as any relevant church events.

BIBLE STUDY

- to recognize the presence of an unseen world that parallels our physical world
- to understand the pointlessness of pursuing the values of the world
- to uncover the three elements of the world's system that work against God's purposes

LIFE CHANGE

- to learn to recognize the world's values and attitudes by making a list of the values we see as we watch TV shows or movies this week
- to learn contentment in our spending habits by developing a monthly spending budget
- to gain a greater understanding of our identity in Christ by reading God's Word every day

Icebreaker   (10-15 minutes)

INTRODUCE THE ICEBREAKER ACTIVITY: The students have been given instructions in their books.

After the Icebreaker say something like, "All around us there are things taking place that we usually overlook. This includes the spiritual world as well as the physical. Today we will see how the world's value system can subtly infiltrate our lives and affect our choices."

Hand out the Prayer/Praise Report. A sample copy is on pages 158-159. Have people write down prayer requests and praises. Then have the prayer coordinator collect the report and make copies for use during the Caring Time.

Explaining the Unseen. The unseen activities listed below are often taken for granted, and we usually don't give much thought to how they occur. Have each member of your group choose one of the following, often unexplained activities and explain how it works. (Even if you don't know for sure, you will want to take a guess!)

- ☐ how electricity works
- ☐ how an airplane flies
- ☐ how the moon controls tides
- ☐ how antibiotics fight infection
- ☐ how a flower grows
- ☐ how a microwave heats food
- ☐ how a thunderstorm develops
- ☐ how a computer processes information
- ☐ how the human brain works

notes:

**LEARNING FROM
THE BIBLE**

1 JOHN 2:15–17

2:24–27

Have a member of
the class, selected
ahead of time, read
aloud the passages
from 1 John.

Bible Study (30-45 minutes)

The Scripture for this week:

¹⁵Do not love the world or anything in the world. If anyone loves the world, the love of the Father is not in him. ¹⁶For everything in the world—the cravings of sinful man, the lust of his eyes and the boasting of what he has and does—comes not from the Father but from the world. ¹⁷The world and its desires pass away, but the man who does the will of God lives forever. ...

²⁴See that what you have heard from the beginning remains in you. If it does, you also will remain in the Son and in the Father. ²⁵And this is what he promised us—even eternal life.

²⁶I am writing these things to you about those who are trying to lead you astray. ²⁷As for you, the anointing you received from him remains in you, and you do not need anyone to teach you. But as his anointing teaches you about all things and as that anointing is real, not counterfeit—just as it has taught you, remain in him.

notes:

Summarize these introductory remarks. Be sure to include the underlined information, which gives the answers to the student book questions (provided in the margin).

...about today's session (5 minutes)

READING THE DEFENSE

In football, the goal of the offense is to get the ball into the end zone and score touchdowns. This is usually not an easy task. The problem is the presence of an opposing force on every play. This force is called the defense. The 11 players on the defensive side of the ball are doing all they can to prevent the offense from moving the ball down the field and scoring. As a result, one of the first things a football coach does to prepare his team to play is to teach his assistant coaches and players how to "read" the defense on every play. The most successful offenses in football are the ones that recognize the defense's tendencies and strategies and learn to counteract them. A good quarterback sometimes changes the play the offense is planning to run because he reads something in the defense that he didn't expect. He changes the plan and executes another play that will be more successful against that defensive alignment.

How can we draw a parallel between serving God and playing football?

As we seek to make a difference in this world for God, we discover that the task is not always easy. Today's session will show us the tendencies and strategies of a spiritual "defensive force" that opposes God's people and their work for His kingdom. In order for us to be successful in making wise decisions, we must learn to read the world's "defense" and understand the strategies that are aimed at defeating us. We must recognize the world's values and how they work against God's purposes. Then we will be able to change our "play" when necessary to lead a victorious Christian life.

What will we gain from understanding the world's strategies?

notes:

11

Remain in groups of 6–8 people, in a horseshoe configuration.

In this small group session, students will be responding to the following questions that will help them share their stories in terms of John's words about loving the world in 1 John 2:15–17, 24–27.

Have the students explore these questions together.

Identifying with the Story (5-7 minutes)

1. As a teenager, which of the following was your greatest "love"?

☐ cars   ☐ sports
☐ academics   ☐ leisure time
☐ a guy I dated   ☐ a girl I dated
  (or wanted to)   (or wanted to)
☐ a movie star   ☐ a rock star
☐ partying   ☐ money
☐ other:_____

2. If our group watched you stroll through a shopping mall, which of the following stores would you most likely be seen going into?

☐ sporting goods store   ☐ music store
☐ computer store   ☐ bookstore
☐ pet store   ☐ furniture store
☐ arts and crafts store   ☐ clothing store
☐ kitchen appliance and accessory store
☐ other:_____

3. Of all your material possessions, which would be the most difficult to give up?

☐ my house   ☐ my stereo system
☐ my car   ☐ my TV
☐ my computer   ☐ my clothes
☐ other:_____

notes:

today's session (15-20 minutes)

Share with your class the following information, which you may modify according to your own perspectives and teaching needs. The answers to the student book questions (provided in the margin to the left of the leader's text) are underlined.

Have you ever noticed that our society readily accepts certain attitudes, perspectives, and values as the standard for how life is best lived? These values arise in a subtle fashion, forming attitudes in our minds about sex, money, relationships, and other key areas of life. We see these values emerging in many segments of our society such as magazine advertisements, TV commercials, TV shows, movies, music, and books. For example, if you spend just a few minutes watching any popular situation comedy on TV, you will most likely observe the value that premarital sex is an accepted way to happiness. These ideas, values, and perspectives don't exist by accident. Today we'll learn there's an unseen world that parallels our physical world generating these philosophies. Many Christians overlook this reality. But just by observing the state of our families, many of our churches, and our communities, it's obvious that something is working against God's people. Many believers just can't pinpoint what or who is the source.

1

What analogy was used to describe the unseen world that opposes the work of Christians?

This unseen world is similar to the presence of unseen germs before the invention of the microscope. Doctors knew something was wreaking havoc with people's lives, but they didn't know what it was. As a result, they experienced great difficulty trying to find cures and medicines that would treat and heal illness and disease. They were trying to treat something they couldn't see and cure something they didn't understand. Unless we become aware of this unseen world and seek to understand its strategies, our attempts to combat it will likely be as futile.

Through today's Scripture passage in 1 John, we will seek to uncover the truth about this unseen world that many Christians ignore and that society unknowingly embraces. We will examine the time-tested tactics and ploys that have successfully led believers away from God's truth through the years. We can be sure that our enemy's strategy will be no different with us than what the early church faced.

What Is the "World"?

In 1 John 2:15–17, John uses the Greek word *kosmos* that is translated "world." In Greek literature, this word meant an order, system, or organization. This word is used in the New Testament to describe a system that is designed to turn people's hearts against God and His truth.

What does John mean when he talks about the "world"?

Politically correct

The world's system consists of all the attitudes, perspectives, and thoughts that we find commonplace in the workplace and home. Peer Believing and living by this system comes easily for many of us. Pressure Everyone around us seems to be making the same decisions based

13

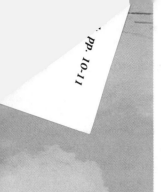

today's session (cont'd)

on the same values and so it appears to be the logical, right way to go. The world's system looks natural because it permeates our society. The problem we face is that, in contrast, God's way seems so unnatural. It doesn't make sense, because the world's system has been so ingrained in our thinking.

What is the inevitable result of following the world's system of values?

If taken to its logical extreme, going with the flow of the world's way of thinking will result in problems such as chemical dependency, poor financial decisions, moral failures, and the destruction of families. The purpose of the world's system is the destruction of those God loves most. The world's system never delivers on its false promises. In 1 John 2:15–17, John gives us an overview of this world system.

In verse 15, John warns: "Do not love the world." He's not talking about the people of the world or the created world. John urges us not to embrace or wholeheartedly surrender to the world. When he says we should not love the world or "anything in the world," he's not referring to things but rather to the values and assumptions we find at work in the world's system.

He then says in verse 15, "If anyone loves the world, the love of the Father is not in him." If we get caught up in the world's system and embrace it, there's a problem. John emphasizes that we can't love God and the world's ways at the same time. Many Christians think they can. You may have fond affection or feelings for some of God's truth, but we can't love God if we are living for the world. Could you imagine a husband informing his wife that he really enjoys spending time with another woman and expecting his wife to be happy?

According to verse 16, what are the three elements of the world's system?

In verse 16, John peels back a layer of the world's system to look at the unseen forces that are at work in the world. He puts "everything in the world" into three categories. First, John mentions the "cravings of sinful man." These are the internal desires that control the words we say, what we see with our eyes, and the desires that we shouldn't pursue. John is showing us that we have internal cravings or desires influencing us to pursue those things we know are wrong. We live in a world that feeds these desires constantly.

The second thing in the world that John warns us against is "the lust of his eyes." This is the desire for the accumulation of things that we don't need. This is what happens when we open a catalog or walk through a shopping mall. We see something we want but don't need. We didn't even know we wanted it until we placed our eyes on it. The result is we buy things we don't need. Not only can "the lust of [the] eyes" result in materialism and growing debt, it can also influence us to pursue relationships that aren't healthy. Men fall into this trap because they are visual in nature. A man sees an attractive woman and if his guard is down, he can be drawn into pursuing an adulterous relationship. Men are at high risk for pornography addiction because of "the lust of his eyes."

The third thing in the world that John warns us against is "the boasting of what he has and does." This is the tendency to hinge our identity on our profession and our possessions instead of who we are in Christ. We love the world when we define our lives by what we do and by what we own.

John reminds us that if we are going to love God, we must move beyond allowing our lives to be controlled by these three things. We are victims of the world's system if we define our lives by them and allow ourselves to be led astray (v. 26). In the back of our minds, we all know where these pursuits will end and that they are counterfeit (v. 27), but we pursue them anyway because it's all we know! We think the outcome in our lives will be different.

John wanted to make it clear that God is not the source of the world's system, stating that it "comes not from the Father" (v. 16). We still get mad at God because we think He is to blame somehow. John points out that the attitudes and perspectives that wreak havoc in our lives are not from God. They come from the world. John goes on to say that, "The world and its desires pass away" (v. 17a). He reveals the temporary nature of the world's system and the futility associated with following its false promises. Then he reminds us to place our hopes on the things that will last far beyond this life. "But the man who does the will of God lives forever" (v. 17b).

Basically, John wonders why anyone would want to spend his or her whole life driven by worldly attitudes and values that he or she is going to outlive. We may look back on those things when our lives are through and wonder why we based our lives and critical decisions on those values. The realization of the futility of the world's system can be readily seen at funerals. In those moments of grief, we see more clearly than usual this life for what it really is. We see that the only values that really matter are the ones that transcend this life into eternity. The call of our heavenly Father is for us to live in this world but not to be "of the world." Let's seek to follow His call and love Him more than this world. Let's "remain in the Son and in the Father" and look to the ultimate reward of eternal life (vv. 24–25).

What do funerals remind us about the world's values?

notes:

⟨horseshoe icon⟩ **Remain in groups of 6–8 people, in a horseshoe configuration.**

In this small-group session, students will be applying the lessons of the text to their own lives through the following questions.

The students were asked (in the student book) to choose an answer for each question and explain why.

✚

Learning from the Story (5-7 minutes)

1. Pick one example of "the cravings of sinful man" that you see prevalent in society. Discuss the false promises behind this example.

   ☐ alcoholism   ☐ drug addiction
   ☐ overeating   ☐ gambling
   ☐ other:_____

2. Pick one example of "the lust of his eyes" that you see prevalent in society. Discuss the false promises behind this example.

   ☐ materialism   ☐ adultery
   ☐ growing debt   ☐ pornography addiction
   ☐ other:_____

3. Pick one example of "the boasting of what he has and does" that you see prevalent in society. Discuss the false promises behind this example.

   ☐ selfishness   ☐ greed
   ☐ pride   ☐ unethical ambition in the workplace
   ☐ other:_____

notes:

16

life change lessons (5-7 minutes)

Share with the class the following thoughts on how the lessons of this text might be applied today. The answers to the student book questions (provided in the margin) are underlined unless the question requires a personal answer.

When is it easy to make wrong choices?

What are three actions you can take to help you combat any allegiance to the world's values, attitudes, and perspectives?

When making decisions, we bring into the mix our own assumptions about what is true or worthwhile. It is easy to make wrong choices when we don't take the time to examine our presuppositions and compare them with the truth of God's Word. Unless we take some proactive steps in resisting the world's value system, we will eventually embrace what the world naturally and consistently tells us. Here are some specific actions we can take to begin removing any attachment we may have to the world's values, attitudes, and perspectives:

1. LEARN TO RECOGNIZE THE WORLD'S VALUES AND ATTITUDES BY MAKING A LIST OF THE VALUES YOU SEE AS YOU WATCH TV SHOWS OR MOVIES THIS WEEK. Without realizing it, you can allow the world's value system to permeate your mind on a regular basis. If this goes unchecked, you'll eventually begin to live your life based on those values. This is a very subtle process, one that can happen without you realizing it.

2. LEARN CONTENTMENT IN YOUR SPENDING HABITS BY DEVELOPING A MONTHLY SPENDING BUDGET. You have two choices concerning the way you handle your money. You can spend your time wondering where it went, or planning where it goes. The latter is the better choice. A budget is nothing more than "planned spending." Start by determining how much money you make in a month. Then determine how much you give for tithing, savings investments, and monthly bills. If you have any left over, this is called disposable income. This is money you have a choice in how you spend. Make sure you do not exceed this amount in a month. By following this process, you can learn to spend within your means and make wiser financial decisions, especially as you stroll down the mall and see something you want. This is one way to resist the urge John refers to as "the lust of his eyes."

3. GAIN A GREATER UNDERSTANDING OF YOUR IDENTITY IN CHRIST BY READING GOD'S WORD ON A DAILY BASIS. You need to become familiar with your identity as a child of God. When you begin to learn what God's Word has to say about your place and security in Christ, you can ground your identity in being a loved and valued child of God, instead of in your possessions or professions. You must follow the instruction of the apostle Paul in Romans 12:2 to "not conform any longer to the pattern of this world, but be transformed by the renewing of your mind."

notes:

Caring Time (15-20 minutes)

This is the time for developing and expressing your caring for each other by praying for one another. Thank God for the truth of His Word and ask Him to break each group member of any unhealthy attachments to the world that are hindering his or her effectiveness in serving Christ. Also, pray for the concerns that are listed on the Prayer/Praise Report.

We're going to pray for one another now. Anyone who is comfortable doing so may pray aloud. The rest of you may talk to God silently. Please remember to pray for the requests and concerns those in your group mentioned earlier.

CARING TIME
Remain in groups of 6–8 people, in a horseshoe configuration.

Hand out the Prayer/ Praise Report to the entire group. Ask each subgroup to pray for the empty chair. Pray specifically for God to guide you to someone to bring next week to fill that chair.

After a sufficient time of prayer in subgroups, close in a corporate prayer. Say, "Next week we will talk about: 'Choosing to Stand Firm.'"

Remind participants of the daily Scripture readings and reflective questions found on page 20.

notes:

Reference Notes

Use these notes to gain further understanding
of the text as you study on your own.

1 JOHN 2:15
unconditional love

love. The Greek word used for love in this verse is *agape*. It describes a love that is unconditional and committed. This is the same kind of love God shows His children.

world. The Greek word John uses here is *kosmos*, and it means that which is alienated from God and is contrary to who God is. It refers to a pagan culture that has abandoned God.

1 JOHN 2:16
the world

cravings. That part of human nature which demands gratification—be it for sexual pleasure, luxury, possessions, expensive food, whatever.

lust of his eyes. Greed that is aroused by sight. A person sees something and wants it. (For examples of this see Genesis 3:6; Joshua 7:21; and 2 Samuel 11:2–4.)

boasting. Pride in one's possessions; an attitude of arrogance because one has acquired so much. In its original Greek usage, this word referred to a man who claimed to be important because he had achieved so much when, in fact, he really had done very little.

1 JOHN 2:17
eternal realities

pass away. To give oneself over to the love of the world is foolish because the world with its values and goods is already passing away (1 John 2:8).

lives forever. In contrast to those who live for the moment are those who give themselves to eternal, unchanging realities.

1 JOHN 2:24
remain in truth

See that. John now issues a command. In the face of the lies of the antichrists they are to remain faithful to the Word of God.

what you have heard from the beginning. As an antidote to false teaching, John urges his readers to let the original message that they heard right from the start of their Christian lives control their perspective.

remain. John's point is that when they remain in the truth, they will remain in fellowship with God.

1 JOHN 2:26
private doctrines

lead you astray. Those who left the church were not content to simply form their own fellowship based on their private doctrines. Instead, they actively sought to make converts from among the Christian community.

1 JOHN 2:27
the Holy Spirit

his anointing. The ultimate safeguard against false teaching is the Word of God. This is conveyed to our hearts by the Holy Spirit with whom we have been anointed.

notes:

Session

2

Choosing to Stand Firm

Prepare for the Session

	READINGS	REFLECTIVE QUESTIONS
Monday	Ephesians 6:10–11	What scheme of the devil has given you the most trouble in the past?
Tuesday	Ephesians 6:12–13	What are the most common struggles you experience in your relationships?
Wednesday	Ephesians 6:14	What are you currently doing to help yourself stand firm in God's truth?
Thursday	Ephesians 6:15	Whose life are you currently investing in for the purpose of sharing Christ?
Friday	Ephesians 6:16	In what area of your life do you need more faith?
Saturday	Ephesians 6:17	Find a Scripture verse that will help you in the area where you are most tempted.*
Sunday	Ephesians 6:18	How does prayer keep you strong against the enemy's attacks?

notes:

* If you don't have a Bible or are having trouble finding a verse, call the person who invited you to this class or contact the class facilitator.

2

OUR GOALS FOR THIS SESSION ARE:

☙ In groups of 6–8, gather people in a horseshoe configuration.

Make sure everyone has a name tag.

Take time to share information on class parties that are coming up as well as any relevant church events.

INTRODUCE THE ICEBREAKER ACTIVITY: The students have been given instructions in their books.

After the Icebreaker say something like, "As we look back on the tough battles we have fought, we may feel like weary soldiers. Whether we know it or not, we are warriors in a spiritual battle for our souls. Today we will discuss how to prepare for that battle by putting on the armor of God."

Hand out the Prayer/Praise Report. A sample copy is on pages 158-159. Have people write down prayer requests and praises. Then have the prayer coordinator collect the report and make copies for use during the Caring Time.

BIBLE STUDY	• to recognize that the source of our struggles is spiritual in nature
	• to learn what pieces of spiritual armor are necessary for withstanding the devil's schemes
	• to understand how to put on the full armor of God
LIFE CHANGE	• to memorize Scripture verses dealing with the temptation that troubles us the most
	• to cultivate a relationship with someone for the purpose of sharing Christ with him or her
	• to develop a prayer list to aid us in praying consistently for the people God has brought into your lives

 Icebreaker (10-15 minutes)

Fighting Battles. Which of the following branches of the military most closely describes the toughest battle you have faced in your life? Complete the statement in a way that creatively describes your battle.

☐ Army—"I was marching in the wrong direction of _____."

☐ Navy—"I was drowning in a sea of _____."

☐ Air Force—"I was hit without warning by the bomb of _____."

☐ Marines—"I went through a tough transition from the Sea of _____ to the Land of _____."

☐ Coast Guard—"I was drifting into the dangerous waters of _____."

notes:

LEARNING FROM THE BIBLE

EPHESIANS 6:10–18

Have two members of the class, selected ahead of time, read the passage from Ephesians. Ask one person to read verses 10–13 and the other to read verses 14–17. Then have the whole class read verse 18 out loud together.

Bible Study   (30-45 minutes)

The Scripture for this week:

¹⁰Be strong in the Lord and in his mighty power. ¹¹Put on the full armor of God so that you can take your stand against the devil's schemes. ¹²For our struggle is not against flesh and blood, but against the rulers, against the authorities, against the powers of this dark world and against the spiritual forces of evil in the heavenly realms. ¹³Therefore put on the full armor of God, so that when the day of evil comes, you may be able to stand your ground, and after you have done everything, to stand. ¹⁴Stand firm then, with the belt of truth buckled around your waist, with the breastplate of righteousness in place, ¹⁵and with your feet fitted with the readiness that comes from the gospel of peace. ¹⁶In addition to all this, take up the shield of faith, with which you can extinguish all the flaming arrows of the evil one. ¹⁷Take the helmet of salvation and the sword of the Spirit, which is the word of God. ¹⁸And pray in the Spirit on all occasions with all kinds of prayers and requests. With this in mind, be alert and always keep on praying for all the saints.

Summarize these introductory remarks. Be sure to include the underlined information, which gives the answers to the student book questions (provided in the margin).

Why do sports organizations require the use of protective gear for their athletes?

Why do you think Jesus wants His children to wear spiritual armor?

...about today's session (5 minutes)

PUTTING ON YOUR EQUIPMENT

Can you imagine being asked to play in an NFL football game without a helmet or pads? The hospital would surely be the next stop for anyone who tried to take that risk. Sports that involve a high degree of physical contact and the potential for injury typically require carefully planned protective gear for its athletes. <u>The organizers of the sport recognize the potential for danger and seek to prevent injury as much as possible.</u>

Similarly, as we seek to advance the gospel and do the work of God's kingdom, we will face spiritual opposition. Today's session focuses on the equipment needed to protect us from the enemy in our war and to keep us out of the hospital! We'll examine the spiritual armor that Paul describes in Ephesians 6:10–18 and learn how <u>to be wise in handling the struggles that God's children encounter.</u> We'll also share some personal steps to take <u>to help us stand firm in our faith.</u>

notes:

2

Ⓤ Remain in groups of 6–8 people, in a horseshoe configuration.

In this small-group session, students will be responding to the following questions that will help them share their stories in terms of Paul's words about putting on the armor of God in Ephesians 6:10–18.

Have the students explore these questions together.

Identifying with the Story (5-7 minutes)

1. As a teenager, which of the following did you "wrestle" with the most?

☐ parental authority   ☐ self-esteem
☐ academics   ☐ social confidence
☐ siblings   ☐ physical appearance
☐ having reliable transportation
☐ other:_____

2. Complete the following sentence: "Looking back over my life, I should have put on some protective armor when ..."

☐ I tried out for that sport.
☐ I got my driver's license.
☐ I talked back to my parents.
☐ I learned how to ride a bicycle.
☐ I got into a fight with _____.
☐ I played on the school playground.
☐ Other:_____

3. What "scheme" do you sense the devil trying to use in your life right now?

today's session (15-20 minutes)

Share with your class the following information, which you may modify according to your own perspectives and teaching needs. The answers to the student book questions (provided in the margin to the left of the leader's text) are underlined.

If our true struggles are not against "flesh and blood," what is the source of the struggles that Christians commonly face?

Why do you think the devil seeks to attack the relationships of Christians?

In our passage today, the apostle Paul addresses the inevitable struggles that Christians face as they try to live out God's purposes in this world. In verse 12, Paul writes that "our struggle is not against flesh and blood." What may seem like relationship problems is really more than what meets the eye. Paul knew that his readers needed some encouragement because of the opposition they were facing for their faith. In John 16:33 Jesus told his disciples, " 'In this world you will have trouble.' " Paul recognized this fact and wanted to help his readers put their struggles into perspective. He instructed them to remain faithful to God and remain standing no matter what difficulties might come their way. He wanted his readers to be prepared and equipped to endure the struggles they would inevitably experience with others. Paul makes it clear that there's something evil behind the scenes working against us and our relationships.

In verse 11 Paul encourages us as believers to take our stand against "the devil's schemes." The devil, also known in Scripture as Satan, is the personality behind evil who is scheming to destroy our lives. His primary strategy targets our relationships with others and our relationship with God. He knows that relationships hold the key to God's work in this world. He knows that God is in the business of reconciling the broken relationship between Himself and mankind through Jesus Christ. The enemy also knows that the health of relationships between spouses, family members, church members, and neighbors is a vital element in God's work.

We may think our struggle is against "flesh and blood," but Paul wants us to recognize that our primary struggle is spiritual in nature. Every relationship has a spiritual component. Our relationship problems are, in essence, spiritual problems. What would happen if your boss, friend, or coworker with whom you hadn't been getting along well came to know Christ? You would most likely experience a difference in your relationship.

So, who is carrying out the "devil's schemes"? In verse 12, Paul writes that our struggles are "against the rulers, against the authorities, against the powers of this dark world and against the spiritual forces of evil in the heavenly realms." There is a spiritual battle that rages in us and around us. We're tempted to think only of what we can see around us with our physical eyes. The reality is that there are evil forces working that we cannot see.

In verse 13 Paul instructs his readers to "put on the full armor of God." Here, Paul uses the analogy of the equipment that a Roman soldier would wear when entering battle. By using this imagery, Paul reinforces the truth that our struggles originate in a spiritual battle that rages around us. There are times we may not feel like we're involved in any kind of warfare, but even if we're unaware whether or not we are in a battle personally, we can see it in the lives of others. Whether it's marriages breaking apart or children rebelling against their parents, all around us relationships are under attack by the enemy. In some stages of life, we're very aware that we're in spiritual warfare and in other stages we are not. Paul wanted to make sure his readers were not caught off guard.

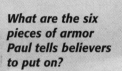

What are the six pieces of armor Paul tells believers to put on?

In verse 14 Paul gives the instruction to, "Stand firm then, with <u>the belt of truth</u> buckled around your waist." The first piece of armor that a Roman soldier put on was the belt. It was underneath his armor and held his sword in place. Paul wants us to make sure the first piece of armor we put on every day is the belt of truth. Satan's primary way of fighting is by getting people to believe lies. The problem is that sometimes his lies sound like truth. For example, Eve heard the serpent say something that sounded right, but in reality it was a well-crafted lie of the enemy. We, as believers, have God's truth in His written Word that helps us stay sensitive to what is truth and what isn't. Jesus used the truth of Scripture to combat Satan's lies during the 40 days that Jesus spent in the wilderness. It's up to each of us to renew our minds to what is true and become sensitive to what is not true as we encounter the lies of the enemy.

The next piece of spiritual armor to be put in place is the "<u>breastplate of righteousness</u>" (v. 14). The breastplate was the largest piece of armor that a soldier wore. Satan often attacks our character and our identity in Christ. The breastplate not only protected the soldier's vital organs, it also displayed which side of the battle he was on. God's righteousness protects our hearts and ensures God's approval. At the moment of conversion, we are given the gift of righteousness. That is, right standing before God, the status of all Christians. When the Father sees us, he sees the righteousness of Jesus Christ. We must remind ourselves daily of this truth—God has given us the gift of righteousness through Christ. As God's children we are to be committed to doing what is right and to desire to live out that righteousness, even when it is difficult.

In verse 15 Paul writes that we're to have our "<u>feet fitted with the readiness that comes from the gospel of peace</u>." Paul is referring to the <u>shoes that a Roman soldier wore</u>. The enemy wants us to become content with self-centered pursuits instead of taking the good news about Jesus wherever we go. As Christians, we should always be ready to leave footprints of the story of Jesus wherever we go and wherever we live. We should begin to work our way into

today's session (cont'd)

people's lives for the purpose of sharing Christ with them. This will happen when we are willing to do whatever God wants us to do, no matter what He requests of us.

Paul then challenges his readers to "take up the shield of faith, with which you can extinguish all the flaming arrows of the evil one" (v. 16). A Roman soldier's shield was large enough for a soldier to hide behind. It was designed to extinguish flying arrows that were dipped in tar and set on fire. Paul relates this shield to faith. A soldier trusted that the shield was sturdy enough to protect him from flaming arrows. Then he wasn't afraid to hide behind it. Satan's flaming arrows are those temptations, insults, and discouraging words we face daily. If we are not protecting ourselves with faith in God, the enemy's arrows can harm our ability to serve Him and weaken our faith in God's ability to make something good come out of bad situations or experiences and to fulfill His promises.

The last piece of protective armor that Paul instructs his readers to use is the "helmet of salvation." The helmet of a Roman soldier covered his head and was a symbol of military victory. The enemy tries to render us ineffective in our work for God's kingdom by making us unsure of our ultimate victory through Christ. We should remind ourselves often that we have already been rescued by Jesus and have already won the victory through Him.

What is the only offensive weapon Paul mentions in his list of a Roman soldier's equipment? How do you think we should use it?

The last image that Paul uses is "the sword of the Spirit, which is the word of God" (v. 17). The sword is the only offensive weapon in this list of armor. There are times when we need to take the offensive against Satan. Even before we come under attack, we can arm ourselves with Scripture by reading it on a regular basis and memorizing the specific passages of Scripture dealing with the areas of temptation that we go head-to-head with every day.

Paul concludes by emphasizing the importance of prayer in our struggles and attacks from the enemy. He reminds us that our ability to prevail in spiritual warfare comes from God's power and not our own. Paul started with this admonition in verse 10: "Finally, be strong in the Lord and in his mighty power." In verse 18 he concludes with a similar thought of dependence on God, "And pray in the Spirit on all occasions with all kinds of prayers and requests. With this in mind, be alert and always keep on praying for all the saints."

What role should prayer play in our ability to endure the "flaming arrows" of the devil?

✚

↻ **Remain in groups of 6–8 people, in a horseshoe configuration.**

In this small-group session, students will be applying the lessons of the text to their own lives through the following questions.

The students were asked (in the student book) to choose an answer for each question and explain why.

Learning from the Story (5-7 minutes)

1. Of the spiritual armor that Paul lists, which one do you have trouble wearing consistently?

   ☐ **"belt of truth"**—trusting in God's truth more than the world's lies

   ☐ **"breastplate of righteousness"**—trusting in Christ's righteousness as my own

   ☐ **"feet fitted with ... readiness"**—faithfully telling others about Jesus

   ☐ **"shield of faith"**—trusting in what God promises more than what sin promises

   ☐ **"helmet of salvation"**—remembering that I have experienced ultimate victory in Christ

   ☐ **"sword of the Spirit"**—reading and knowing the Bible

2. In verse 18, Paul gives instructions for our prayer lives. Which of Paul's instructions would improve your personal prayer life the most?

   ☐ pray with more frequency—"on all occasions"

   ☐ pray with more variety—"with all kinds of prayers and requests"

   ☐ pray more unselfishly—"for all the saints"

3. In which area of your walk with Christ do you need the most help "standing firm"? What can this group do to help you?

2

notes:

Share with the class the following thoughts on how the lessons of this text might be applied today. The answers to the student book questions (provided in the margin) are underlined unless the question requires a personal answer.

Why is identifying and preparing for the "flaming arrows" of Satan a difficult task?

What are three steps you can take to begin putting on the spiritual armor Paul describes?

life change lessons (5-7 minutes)

Because our struggles are spiritual and unseen in nature, identifying and preparing for Satan's flaming arrows can be difficult. Here are some steps you can take to begin putting on the spiritual armor that Paul describes:

1. MEMORIZE SCRIPTURE VERSES DEALING WITH THE TEMPTATION THAT TROUBLES YOU THE MOST. Memorizing Scripture seems like drudgery to many believers, not to mention hard work. However, it can actually be fun if you find a partner to memorize the same verse(s) with you. An easy way to memorize verse(s) is to record them on note cards and put them in conspicuous places, such as on the dashboard of your car, where you will see the verse(s) often.

2. CULTIVATE A RELATIONSHIP WITH SOMEONE FOR THE PURPOSE OF SHARING CHRIST WITH HIM OR HER. If you don't have someone whom you are currently investing time in to help him or her begin a relationship with Christ, then pray that God will send someone into your life. Find common ground with that person and then begin to show genuine concern for him or her. Pray for the person consistently and be sensitive to the Spirit's timing for when to share Christ with him or her.

3. DEVELOP A PRAYER LIST TO AID YOU IN PRAYING CONSISTENTLY FOR THE PEOPLE GOD HAS BROUGHT INTO YOUR LIFE. A prayer list is a way to be consistent in praying for individuals that God has brought to your attention. This list could include family members, non-Christian friends, coworkers, neighbors, ministers, church members, etc. When God answers a particular need in a person's life, note that on your list, letting it be a reminder of how God is working.

notes:

CARING TIME
Remain in groups of 6–8 people, in a horseshoe configuration.

Hand out the Prayer/Praise Report to the entire group. Ask each subgroup to pray for the empty chair. Pray specifically for God to guide you to someone to bring next week to fill that chair.

After a sufficient time of prayer in subgroups, close in a corporate prayer. Say, "Next week we will talk about: 'Choosing Wisdom in Relationships.' "

Remind participants of the daily Scripture readings and reflective questions found on page 32.

Caring Time   (15-20 minutes)

Take time to pray for one another and for your own special concerns. Have group members pray especially for help in wearing their spiritual armor to protect them from the enemy's attack. Also, remember to pray about the concerns listed on the Prayer/Praise Report.

Close by thanking God for bringing you together as a group and by asking Him to strengthen each group member, enabling him or her to stand firm against the schemes of the devil.

2

notes:

BIBLE STUDY NOTES

Reference Notes

Use these notes to gain further understanding
of the text as you study on your own.

EPHESIANS 6:10
God's power

be strong…in his mighty power. Paul uses the same three words here as he used in Ephesians 1:19, when he first tried to describe God's indescribable power. In order to wage successful warfare against Satan, the Christian must draw upon God's own power. This is a power outside ourselves from beyond. This is not a natural power generated by the Christian.

EPHESIANS 6:11
God's armor

Put on. It is not enough to rely passively on God's power. The Christian must do something. Specifically, he or she must "put on" God's armor.
full armor. Paul uses the Greek term *panoplia* (from which the English word "panoply" comes), which can be understood as the complete catalog of equipment needed by a soldier.
the devil's schemes. Evil does not operate in the light. It lurks in shadows and strikes unexpectedly, with cleverness and subtlety.

EPHESIANS 6:12
evil powers

the rulers … the authorities … the spiritual forces. By these various titles, Paul names the diverse spiritual forces that rage against humanity. These are intangible spiritual entities whose will is often worked out via concrete historical, economic, political, social, and institutional structures. Part of the call to Christians is to identify the places where these evil powers are at work.
the powers of this dark world. It was no empty boast on Satan's part when, during Jesus' temptations, he claimed to be able to give Him "all the kingdoms of the world" (Matt. 4:8). These "world rulers" have real power, and even though Christ has defeated them, they refuse to concede defeat (though at Christ's second coming they will be forced to do so).
forces of evil. Another characteristic of these supernatural beings is wickedness. They are of the darkness, not of the light.

EPHESIANS 6:13
stand firm

the day of evil. Although Paul may have in mind the final day of judgment, the immediate reference is to those special times of pressure and testing that come to all Christians, during which steadfast resistance of evil is required.
stand your ground. This is the second time Paul has spoken about standing fast (see also v. 11). Twice more, he will urge the same thing (vv. 13–14). This is the basic posture of the Christian in the face of evil: resistance. "Standing firm" is a military image. Paul may well have in mind the fighting position of the Roman legions. Fully-equipped soldiers were virtually invulnerable to an enemy onslaught—unless they panicked and broke ranks. As long as they "stood firm" when the enemy attacked, they would prevail in the long run. Most of all, their equipment, as will be seen in verses 14–17, was designed to enable them to "hold the position." This is the key to resisting evil.

✝

EPHESIANS 6:14–17

All the pieces of armor (except one) are defensive in nature, rather than aggressive in intent. Each piece of armor is used by Paul as a metaphor for what the Christian needs to stand against the dark forces of Satan.

EPHESIANS 6:14
integrity

the belt of truth. This refers to the leather belt on which the Roman soldier hung his sword and by which he secured his tunic and armor (so he would be unimpeded in battle). The "truth" is the inner integrity and sincerity by which the Christian fights evil. Lying and deceit are tactics of the enemy.

the breastplate of righteousness. The breastplate was the major piece of armor for the Roman soldier. Made of metal and leather, it protected his vital organs. "Righteousness" refers to the right standing before God that is the status of the Christian, out of which moral conduct and character emerges.

EPHESIANS 6:15
solid foundation

feet fitted. These are the leather half-boots worn by the Roman legion-naire, with heavy studded soles that enabled him to dig in and resist being pushed out of place.

readiness. This term can be translated as "firmness" or "steadfastness," in which case "the gospel of peace" is understood to provide the solid foundation on which the Christian stands in the fight against evil.

EPHESIANS 6:16
steadfast faith

the shield of faith. The large, oblong shield was constructed of layers of wood on an iron frame which was then covered with linen and hide. When wet, such a shield could absorb "flaming arrows."

flaming arrows. These were pitch-soaked arrows. Their aim was not so much to kill a soldier as to set him aflame and cause him to break rank and create panic.

EPHESIANS 6:17
secure salvation

the helmet of salvation. This heavy, metal head-covering lined with felt or sponge gave substantial protection to the soldier's head from all but the heaviest axe blow. Salvation is like that—but stronger, impenetrable. The sure knowledge that one's salvation is secure—that the outcome of the battle is already known—is the ultimate defense against Satan.

sword. A short, stabbing sword used for personal combat. The sword is the only piece of offensive equipment in the armor. The main task of the Christian is to withstand the onslaught of evil powers, not to attack, except in one way—by telling the Word of God in the power of the Spirit.

EPHESIANS 6:18
indispensable prayer

pray. Paul does not consider prayer a seventh weapon. Rather, it underlies the whole process of spiritual warfare.

in the Spirit. The Bible, the Word of God, is the sword of the Spirit. So, too, prayer is guided by the Spirit. This is, after all, spiritual warfare.

2

notes:

Session

3

Choosing
Wisdom in Relationships

Prepare for the Session

	READINGS	REFLECTIVE QUESTIONS
Monday	James 3:13	How does your life demonstrate that you have wisdom?
Tuesday	James 3:14	Are you harboring bitterness toward someone but pretending that everything's okay?
Wednesday	James 3:15	How does James describe the "wisdom" that doesn't come from God?
Thursday	James 3:16	Is there any selfishness or envy in your life that is causing disorder in any of your relationships?
Friday	James 3:17	How does James describe the wisdom that comes from God?
Saturday	James 3:17	In what ways does your life display the characteristics associated with godly wisdom?
Sunday	James 3:18	Would you consider yourself a peacemaker? If so, why?

notes:

OUR GOALS FOR THIS SESSION ARE:

⋃ In groups of 6–8, gather people in a horseshoe configuration.

Make sure everyone has a name tag.

Take time to share information on class parties that are coming up as well as any relevant church events.

BIBLE STUDY

- to understand the principle of reaping and sowing in our relationships
- to see the negative consequences of living by "earthly" wisdom
- to examine the ways that godly wisdom promotes healthy relationships

LIFE CHANGE

- to assess how wise we are in our relationships according to the six aspects of godly wisdom from James
- to seek forgiveness from those whom we have hurt because we relied on "earthly" wisdom
- to ask God daily for wisdom in becoming a peacemaker in all our relationships

3

lcebreaker (10-15 minutes)

Animal Lover. Take turns sharing which of the following animals most closely describes the way you typically relate to others.

- ☐ Golden Retriever—dependable
- ☐ Lion—intimidating
- ☐ Beaver—hard worker
- ☐ Chameleon—influenced by others
- ☐ Porcupine—hard to get close to
- ☐ Turtle—persistent
- ☐ Dove—peacemaker
- ☐ Lamb—trusting
- ☐ Deer—not trusting
- ☐ Ant—team player

INTRODUCE THE ICEBREAKER ACTIVITY: The students have been given instructions in their books.

After the Icebreaker say something like, "We all have different ways of approaching relationships. We're influenced by many factors, including our personalities and past experiences. Today we'll see how God wants us to relate to others and how we need His wisdom to do so."

Hand out the Prayer/Praise Report. A sample copy is on pages 158-159. Have people write down prayer requests and praises. Then have the prayer coordinator collect the report and make copies for use during the Caring Time.

notes:

LEARNING FROM
THE BIBLE

JAMES 3:13–18

Have a member of
the class, selected
ahead of time,
read the passage
from James.

Bible Study   (30-45 minutes)

The Scripture for this week:

¹³*Who is wise and understanding among you? Let him show it by his good life, by deeds done in the humility that comes from wisdom. ¹⁴But if you harbor bitter envy and selfish ambition in your hearts, do not boast about it or deny the truth. ¹⁵Such "wisdom" does not come down from heaven but is earthly, unspiritual, of the devil. ¹⁶For where you have envy and selfish ambition, there you find disorder and every evil practice.*

¹⁷*But the wisdom that comes from heaven is first of all pure; then peace-loving, considerate, submissive, full of mercy and good fruit, impartial and sincere. ¹⁸Peacemakers who sow in peace raise a harvest of righteousness.*

Summarize these
introductory remarks.
Be sure to include
the underlined
information, which
gives the answers
to the student book
questions (provided
in the margin).

What are two "game plans" people can use in relationship building?

...about today's session (5 minutes)

CHOOSING A GOOD GAME PLAN

Successful football teams develop what they call a "game plan." It takes into account the other team's strengths and weaknesses as well as their own. Coaches work diligently to develop offensive plays and defensive alignments that will give their team the greatest chance for success against the team they are playing next.

Each of us has a "game plan" for how we approach the relationships in our lives, whether we realize it or not. According to the passage we are studying today, there are two "game plans" at our disposal for relating to others. We can build our relationships with earthly wisdom or heavenly wisdom. Our ability to make wise decisions in relationships will depend on the one we choose to follow. The choice we make is critical because of the different personalities we encounter every day. If we took an inventory of all the problems in our lives, we'd most likely discover that many have to do with personality conflicts and strained relationships. And when your relationships are bad, life hurts! Difficult or strained relationships can rise up with a family member, neighbor, or coworker. Many of us have relationships that feel like the trick Wily Fox played on Brer Rabbit. "The fox made a doll out of tar and stuck it on the side of the road. When Rabbit saw the tar baby, he thought it was a person and stopped to visit. It was a one-sided conversation. The tar baby's silence bothered the rabbit. He couldn't stand to be next to someone and not communicate with them. So in his frustration he hit the tar baby and stuck to it. He hit the tar baby again with the other foot and, you guessed it, the other hand got stuck."[1]

How are some relationships in our lives similar to Brer Rabbit's experience with the tar baby?

That's how it is with many of our relationships—<u>we get stuck with someone we can't communicate with.</u> What do we do when that happens? We have a choice. We can approach our relationships with wisdom from the world or with wisdom from God. Today we will discuss how we can be sure to choose God's wisdom in dealing with our relationships.

notes:

3

U Remain in groups of 6–8 people, in a horseshoe configuration.

In this small group session, students will be responding to the following questions that will help them share their stories in terms of James' words about wisdom in James 3:13–18.

Have the students explore these questions together.

Identifying with the Story (5-7 minutes)

1. Finish this sentence with one of the following endings: "As far as relationships go, I spend most of my time ..."

- ☐ saying I'm sorry.
- ☐ giving my opinion.
- ☐ offering encouraging words.
- ☐ listening carefully to what others say.
- ☐ defending myself.
- ☐ trying to impress others.
- ☐ assisting others.
- ☐ expressing my feelings.
- ☐ enduring difficult relationships.
- ☐ other:_____

2. Who do you consider to be the wisest person in your life? What makes you think that way about him or her?

3. What is the wisest decision you've made in the past month and why?

Share with your class the following information which you may modify according to your own perspectives and teaching needs. The answers to the student book questions (provided in the margin) are underlined.

According to verse 18, what is the key to being a "peacemaker" in relationships?

How does James describe wisdom in verse 13?

What are two types of wisdom that James describes in our passage today?

What are six characteristics of the "wisdom that comes from heaven"?

today's session (15-20 minutes)

Every day we plant seeds in our relationships. These seeds can be good or bad. Often, we sow seeds of discouraging words, anger, and destructive criticism and expect to reap good relationships in return. We need to understand the principle of sowing and reaping. In Galatians 6:7–8 we see this principle, "Do not be deceived: God cannot be mocked. A man reaps what he sows. The one who sows to please his sinful nature, from that nature will reap destruction." James tells us in verse 18 that the wise person is someone who sows words, behaviors, and attitudes that promote peaceful relationships: "Peacemakers who sow in peace raise a harvest of righteousness." How can we learn to be wise in our relationships and plant good seeds? In our Scripture passage today, James will tell us that we should base our relationships on godly wisdom instead of "earthly" wisdom.

James begins by defining wisdom. He says that wisdom is not knowledge or intelligence. Wisdom is a lifestyle. In verse 13 he answers his own question: "Who is wise and understanding among you? Let him show it by his good life." Wisdom is evidenced by the way we live. It is especially evident in the character we display in our relationships and the manner in which we get along with others.

The first kind of wisdom James discusses is one that he urges us to avoid. It is the wisdom that the world offers. This wisdom is not really wisdom at all, although many people label it as such. This kind of "wisdom" causes untold problems in our relationships. In verse 16, James shows us that "where you have envy and selfish ambition, there you find disorder and every evil practice." James would ask, "Do you have chaos in your relationships?" If so, he would say that what you're lacking is true wisdom.

The second kind of wisdom James discusses is the "wisdom that comes from heaven." This is the godly wisdom that we need to cultivate. In verse 17, James describes six ways we can demonstrate this kind of wisdom in our lives. The first way is by our integrity. James writes, "The wisdom that comes from heaven is first of all pure." The word for pure means "uncorrupted" or "authentic." If we're wise, we won't try to manipulate others, lie to others, practice deceitfulness, cheat others, or use people for selfish gain. The strongest relationships are built on honesty and realness. A person with integrity seeks to give while a person without integrity seeks to get. A person with integrity is always out for the other person's best interest. Great relationships are built on trust and respect. Living with integrity has tremendous benefits. If we tell the truth and live the truth, we'll never have to remember what we've said or how we've

36

acted. Our words and actions can easily catch up to us, though, when we don't live with integrity.

The second way we can demonstrate godly wisdom is in the way we handle anger. James says that wisdom is "peace-loving." This means that we're not bent on using anger to get our way or win arguments. We all know people who always seem to be looking for a fight. These individuals are not being wise. All of us could probably think of something stupid that we've done or said in anger. We need to control our tempers, because when anger is allowed to go unchecked, we make painful mistakes. Proverbs 14:29 says, "A patient man has great understanding, but a quick-tempered man displays folly."

The third way we show godly wisdom is in the way we respond to the feelings of others. This is an area where many people struggle. James says that wisdom is "considerate." This means that we are gentle, courteous, and mindful of the feelings of others. When we minimize the feelings of others, we can easily crush the spirit of a person. We make the mistake of thinking that if they don't feel the way we feel, their feelings are invalid, illogical, or irrational. Wisdom means that we take seriously the feelings of others and respond with kind words. Proverbs 15:4 says, "The tongue that brings healing is a tree of life, but a deceitful tongue crushes the spirit."

The fourth way we can show godly wisdom in our relationships is in our openness to new ideas or the opinions of others. James says that wisdom is evident in our lives when we are "submissive." This word gives the idea of being "considerate," "open to reason," or "open for discussion." Can other people reason with you? Do you get defensive too easily? Are you open to advice and counsel? Proverbs 12:15 says, "The way of a fool seems right to him, but a wise man listens to advice." If something is true about us, we should listen and learn. If someone says something about us that is false, we should forget it.

The fifth way we can demonstrate godly wisdom is in how we respond to the mistakes of others. James says that wisdom is "full of mercy and good fruit." Being full of mercy means that we give others what they need, not what they deserve. We have a choice— we can "rub it in" and hound others about their past mistakes or we can "rub it out" and forgive them. Proverbs 17:9 says, "He who covers over an offense promotes love, but whoever repeats the matter separates close friends."

The sixth way James describes godly wisdom is with the words "impartial and sincere." We are impartial when we treat everyone the same and avoid showing favorites. We are sincere when we are honest about our weaknesses. This is difficult because we tend to put on our best face before others, especially at church. Earthly wisdom tells us to hide those ugly things in our lives that others probably

today's session (cont'd)

already know about us anyway. We're not wise when we pretend to be perfect, because everyone else can see through our act! The wise person doesn't try to be someone they're not. We are at our best when we focus on being our godly selves. Wisdom is treating everyone the same and being the same person no matter who we're with.

notes:

Remain in groups of 6–8 people, in a horseshoe configuration.

In this small-group session, students will be applying the lessons of the text to their own lives through the following questions.

The students were asked (in the student book) to choose an answer for each question and explain why.

Learning from the Story (5-7 minutes)

1. Why do you think James says we will "find disorder and every evil practice" in our relationships when selfishness and envy are present?

2. Which of the following traits James uses to describe the "wisdom that comes from heaven," most closely describes your healthiest relationship?

   ☐ pure   ☐ submissive
   ☐ peace-loving   ☐ impartial
   ☐ considerate   ☐ sincere
   ☐ full of mercy and good fruit

3. In order to take this passage seriously, what is the first thing you need to do?

   ☐ ask someone to forgive you of an offense
   ☐ tell someone the truth
   ☐ begin listening with an open mind
   ☐ forgive someone you've held a grudge against
   ☐ begin speaking encouraging words
   ☐ other:_____

notes:

Share with the class the following thoughts on how the lessons of this text might be applied today. The answers to the student book questions (provided in the margin) are underlined unless the question requires a personal answer.

Use the following chart to help you determine how wise you are in the way you handle your relationships. (The students have been provided the same chart in their text.)

life change lessons (5-7 minutes) ③

Knowing what is right and having the courage to do what is right are two different things. Whether you've gotten anything out of today's session or not will depend on what you do from now on in your relationships. Remember, you get out of relationships what you put into relationships. A large part of the equation lies in whether we approach them with earthly wisdom or with godly wisdom. Here are some steps you can take that will help you begin the habit of sowing seeds as a peacemaker:

1. ASSESS HOW WISE YOU ARE IN YOUR RELATIONSHIPS ACCORD-ING TO THE SIX ASPECTS OF GODLY WISDOM THAT JAMES GIVES. Use the following chart to help you determine how wise you are in the way you handle your relationships.

Here's how the scale works: **1**—Never; **5**—Occasionally, **10**—Always.

I am honest and pure in my motives.

    1 · 2 · 3 · 4 · 5 · 6 · 7 · 8 · 9 · 10

I control my temper.

    1 · 2 · 3 · 4 · 5 · 6 · 7 · 8 · 9 · 10

I am considerate of others' feelings.

    1 · 2 · 3 · 4 · 5 · 6 · 7 · 8 · 9 · 10

I am open to reason and counsel.

    1 · 2 · 3 · 4 · 5 · 6 · 7 · 8 · 9 · 10

I forgive the mistakes of others easily.

    1 · 2 · 3 · 4 · 5 · 6 · 7 · 8 · 9 · 10

I am impartial and genuine with others.

    1 · 2 · 3 · 4 · 5 · 6 · 7 · 8 · 9 · 10

life change lessons (cont'd)

From whom do you need to seek forgiveness?

2. SEEK FORGIVENESS FROM THOSE YOU HAVE HURT BECAUSE YOU RELIED ON "EARTHLY" WISDOM. Sometimes you may be unaware that your behavior has hurt someone's feelings or harmed a relationship. Is there disorder or "walls" in any of your relationships? Refusal to forgive, jealousy, and selfishness are aspects of earthly wisdom that can destroy relationships. Go to those you have offended and ask their forgiveness. This requires dropping your pride and ego. You not only need the wisdom to know what's right but the courage to do what's right, however uncomfortable or awkward it may be (Matt. 5:23–24).

How do you plan to seek God's wisdom daily so you can begin the habit of sowing seeds as a peacemaker?

3. ASK GOD DAILY FOR WISDOM IN BECOMING A PEACEMAKER IN ALL YOUR RELATIONSHIPS. Relationships sometimes involve complex issues and problems. You won't always know how to respond to your relationships. You need God to show you exactly how to respond because you can't see a clear solution. James 1:5 says, "If any of you lacks wisdom, he should ask God, who gives generously to all without finding fault, and it will be given to him." You need God's wisdom every day as you seek to sow seeds as a peacemaker. In doing so, you'll make wise decisions in the critical moments of your relationships.

notes:

⊙ CARING TIME
Remain in groups of 6–8 people, in a horseshoe configuration.

Hand out the Prayer/ Praise Report to the entire group. Ask each subgroup to pray for the empty chair. Pray specifically for God to guide you to someone to bring next week to fill that chair.

After a sufficient time of prayer in subgroups, close in a corporate prayer. Say, "Next week we will talk about: 'Choosing to Delight in God.'"

Remind participants of the daily Scripture readings and reflective questions found on page 44.

Caring Time   (15-20 minutes)

Remember that this is the time for expressing your caring for each other and for supporting one another in prayer. Take a few minutes for each group member to pray for wisdom concerning a difficult relationship he or she is involved with. Also, pray for the concerns listed on the Prayer/Praise Report.

Conclude your prayer time by reading together the words of Jesus in Matthew 5:7–10:

> *Blessed are the merciful,*
> *for they will be shown mercy.*
> *Blessed are the pure in heart,*
> *for they will see God.*
> *Blessed are the peacemakers,*
> *for they will be called sons of God.*
> *Blessed are those who are persecuted because of righteousness,*
> *for theirs is the kingdom of heaven.*

3

notes:

✝

BIBLE STUDY NOTES

Reference Notes

Use these notes to gain further understanding
of the text as you study on your own.

JAMES 3:13
good deeds

by his good life, by deeds. Understanding, like faith, is shown by *how one lives*. Specifically, understanding is demonstrated by a good life and by good deeds. This is what Jesus taught—and lived (see Matt. 7:15–23).

JAMES 3:14
rivalry

bitter envy. The word translated "bitter" is the same word that was used in verse 12 to describe brackish water unfit for human consumption. It is not applied to zeal (the word translated "envy" is literally *zelos*). Zeal that has gone astray becomes jealousy.

selfish ambition. The word translated here as "selfish ambition" originally meant "those who can be hired to do spinning." Then it came to mean "those who work for pay." It later came to mean "those who work only for what they get out of it" and it was applied to those who sought political office merely for personal gain.

in your hearts. This is the issue: What lies at the core of the person's being?

do not boast about it or deny the truth. Those whose hearts are filled with this sense of rivalry and party spirit should not pretend they are speaking God's wisdom. That merely compounds the wrong.

JAMES 3:15
false wisdom

James uses three terms—each of which is less desirable than the previous one—to describe the true origin of this "non-wisdom." There is "earthly" wisdom that arises out of this world. There is "unspiritual" wisdom that arises out of the "soul" of the person. Neither form of wisdom is necessarily bad, except when it claims to originate with the Spirit of God or violates biblical principles. And then there is wisdom "of the devil" that is not neutral. This is literally, "demon-like"; i.e., that which is possessed even by demons (see James 2:19) or is under the control of evil spirits.

JAMES 3:16–18

James contrasts the lifestyle that emerges from pretend wisdom (v. 16) with that which arises out of true wisdom (vv. 17–18).

JAMES 3:17
true wisdom

pure. The Greek word describes a moral purity.

peace-loving. This is the opposite of envy and ambition. True wisdom produces right relationships between people, which is the root idea behind the word *peace* when it is used in the New Testament.

considerate. This is a very difficult word to translate into English. It has the sense of that "which steps in to correct things when the law itself has become unjust" as Aristotle put it.

submissive. True wisdom is willing to listen, learn, and then yield when persuaded.

full of mercy and good fruit. True wisdom reaches out to the unfortunate in practical ways, a point James never tires of making.

**JAMES 3:17
(cont'd)**

impartial. Literally, "undivided"; that is, true wisdom does not vacillate back and forth. It is the opposite of the wavering person in James 1:6–8.

sincere. True wisdom does not act or pretend. It is honest and genuine.

JAMES 3:18

Peace flows from true wisdom in contrast to the sort of harsh insistence on "truth" that divides people. Those who sow peace reap right actions.

notes:

---

[1] Janet P. Johnson, *Brer Rabbit and the Tar Baby* (Memphis: Troll Assoc., 1997).

Session

4

Choosing to Delight in God

Prepare for the Session

	READINGS	REFLECTIVE QUESTIONS
Monday	Psalm 37:3	Are there areas in your life where you are hesitant to trust God?
Tuesday	Psalm 37:4	Is there anything or anyone in your life that rivals God as your greatest delight?
Wednesday	Psalm 37:4	What condition is placed on God giving you the desires of your heart?
Thursday	Psalm 37:5–6	What does the person who wrote these words call you to do in response to the apparent injustices around you? What will God do?
Friday	Psalm 37:7a	Do you take time each day to be still before God? If not, what is keeping you from doing so?
Saturday	Psalm 37:7b	What is the most obvious area of impatience and worry in your life right now?
Sunday	Psalm 37:7c	What is your usual response to the ungodly who are "successful" in the world's eyes?

notes:

BIBLE STUDY	• to understand what it means to make God the "delight" of our lives
	• to know what it means to wait on God
	• to learn the importance of depending on God after He begins to fulfill our deepest desires
LIFE CHANGE	• to reprioritize our life passions
	• to be faithful in the little things while we wait for greater opportunities
	• to share our testimonies often of how God is giving us the desires of our hearts

Icebreaker   (10-15 minutes)

Just Delightful. Put an "X" on each of the lines below—somewhere between the two extremes—to indicate how you see each of these areas of your life. If time is limited, choose only two or three.

MY JOB IS A:

Drag ·   ·   ·   ·   ·   ·   ·   ·   ·   ·   Delight

DOING YARD WORK IS A:

Drag ·   ·   ·   ·   ·   ·   ·   ·   ·   ·   Delight

SHOPPING IS A:

Drag ·   ·   ·   ·   ·   ·   ·   ·   ·   ·   Delight

WATCHING SPORTS IS A:

Drag ·   ·   ·   ·   ·   ·   ·   ·   ·   ·   Delight

MY TIME ALONE WITH GOD IS A:

Drag ·   ·   ·   ·   ·   ·   ·   ·   ·   ·   Delight

MY CLOSE RELATIONSHIPS ARE A:

Drag ·   ·   ·   ·   ·   ·   ·   ·   ·   ·   Delight

4

Sidebar

OUR GOALS FOR THIS SESSION ARE:

⊌ **In groups of 6–8, gather people in a horseshoe configuration.**

Make sure everyone has a name tag.

Take time to share information on class parties that are coming up as well as any relevant church events.

INTRODUCE THE ICEBREAKER ACTIVITY: The students have been given instructions in their books.

After the Icebreaker say something like, "There are many things in this world we can find delight in, but none bring true satisfaction. Today, we will discuss making God our one, true delight."

Hand out the Prayer/Praise Report. A sample copy is on pages 158-159. Have people write down prayer requests and praises. Then have the prayer coordinator collect the report and make copies for use during the Caring Time.

---

notes:

**LEARNING FROM
THE BIBLE**

PSALM 37:3–9

**Have a class member,
selected ahead of
time, read the
passage from Psalms.**

Bible Study   (30-45 minutes)

The Scripture for this week:

³*Trust in the Lord and do good;*
   dwell in the land and enjoy safe pasture.
⁴*Delight yourself in the Lord*
   and he will give you the desires of your heart.
⁵*Commit your way to the Lord;*
   trust in him and he will do this:
⁶*He will make your righteousness shine like the dawn,*
   the justice of your cause like the noonday sun.
⁷*Be still before the Lord and wait patiently for him;*
   do not fret when men succeed in their ways,
   when they carry out their wicked schemes.
⁸*Refrain from anger and turn from wrath;*
   do not fret—it leads only to evil.
⁹*For evil men will be cut off,*
   but those who hope in the Lord will inherit the land.

notes:

Summarize these
introductory remarks.
Be sure to include
the underlined
information, which
gives the answers
to the student book
questions (provided
in the margin).

...about today's session (5 minutes)

PLAYING FOR THE LOVE OF THE GAME

Much has been written about the huge salaries that professional athletes are paid. Some fans wonder if they play just for the money or because of their love for the game. A movie about baseball, entitled *For the Love of the Game*, depicts an aging pitcher who is pitching the game of his life in the last game of his career. He's not pitching for money but because he loves the game so much. Most athletes discover that their energies are most wisely used when they are funneled onto the playing field. If dedication, practice, and hard work are directed toward the game they love to play, their performance will speak for itself and the big money contracts will eventually come. After all, their agents are paid to handle all of the contract worries.

4

*With what do too
many Christians
become overly
concerned that
keeps them from
making God the
delight of their lives?*

In today's session, we're going to study the principle of making God the delight of our lives. Many Christians become overly concerned with the "stuff" that God can bring them. When our greatest satisfaction is in God, however, our desires in life will be the right ones! Here's a story that brings out this principle.

*How is a dog chasing
its tail similar to
chasing after the
desires of our hearts?*

"A puppy said to a big dog, 'I have mastered philosophy. I have learned that the best thing for a dog is happiness, and that happiness is my tail. Therefore I am chasing it, and when I catch it, I shall have it!' The old dog replied, 'I, too, have judged that happiness is a marvelous thing for a dog, and that happiness indeed resides in my tail. I've noticed that when I chase it, it keeps running away from me, but when I go about my business, it comes after me.' "[1]

We serve God the best when we find our greatest satisfaction in Him and His work. As we delight in God, all our deepest desires will come to fruition.

notes:

⊕

Identifying with the Story (5-7 minutes)

Remain in groups of 6–8 people, in a horseshoe configuration.

In this small group session, students will be responding to the following questions that will help them share their stories in terms of the words of David in Psalm 37.

Have the students explore these questions together.

1. Complete the following statement with the answers that apply to you: "I just love ..."

   ☐ eating ice cream   ☐ watching scary movies
   ☐ talking on the phone   ☐ listening to country music
   ☐ vacationing at the beach   ☐ meeting new people
   ☐ going to live sporting events
   ☐ other:_____

2. Which of the following tests your patience the most?

   ☐ long lines at the grocery store checkout counter
   ☐ rush hour traffic
   ☐ working with a certain coworker
   ☐ poor service at restaurants
   ☐ going on vacation with family
   ☐ long sermons
   ☐ other:_____

3. What job or occupation would you enjoy doing even if you never received a paycheck?

   ☐ golf pro   ☐ youth minister
   ☐ teacher   ☐ musician
   ☐ lifeguard   ☐ game show host
   ☐ other:_____

notes:

today's session (15-20 minutes)

Share with your class the following information which you may modify according to your own perspectives and teaching needs. The answers to the student book questions (provided in the margin) are underlined.

What is the theme of Psalm 37?

What are the two extremes that believers experience concerning God's will?

The theme of Psalm 37 is related to the contrast between the wicked and those who live by God's standards, the righteous. It compares the lives of those who are evil with those who seek to live for God. David addresses such issues as injustice, fairness, and the prosperity of the wicked. When confronted with these issues in our lives, the question of God's will is inevitably raised. Unfortunately, one of the great forms of bondage that many Christians experience revolves around the topic of God's will. In their minds, the idea of God's will is more like a maze than a clear path. Actually, God's will is far simpler than we think. Today we will uncover some principles and truths to revolutionize your life and free you from this mindset.

There are two extremes that Christians experience when confronted with the question of God's will. The first extreme is that believers can become consumed with spiritual paranoia. This happens when they get overly concerned about looking for the missing piece that will make the whole puzzle fit together. They are overly concerned that they'll do the wrong thing and believe that God is watching and waiting for them to mess up so He can "zap" them! That is one end of the spectrum. The other extreme is spiritual ambivalence. This is when people seek to do their best in life and don't worry about God's will. They really don't think that God makes it all that clear anyway, so it doesn't matter to them. They believe it's impossible to know God's will for sure, so they just give up and hope it works out in the end.

In verse 4 of our passage today there's a principle that will help us find a happy medium between these two extremes. David writes, "Delight yourself in the Lord and he will give you the desires of your heart." There's something about the latter part of this verse that sounds good to our ears. We all want to be happy and have our desires met. Some people think God is spending all of His time trying to make our lives miserable. They think God is holding out on them. This is the message the serpent gave to Eve in the Garden of Eden. He basically told them, "If you eat the fruit, you'll experience true happiness." Some people won't tell God the truth about their desires because they believe He'll give them the exact opposite of what they ask. For some reason many believers have a subtle doubt that God will give them the desires of their heart. As we look at verse 4, we notice this verse has two parts. This is a conditional verse with a promise. The condition is that we make knowing and enjoying God our greatest joy and source of satisfaction in our lives. Ask yourself this question: "If someone spent an afternoon with you, would they

4

today's session (cont'd)

know that you have a passion for God?" David is telling us that if we focus on the condition, God will take care of the promise.

Some may think, "Aren't we supposed to have some sort of major spiritual encounter and then God will write His will on the clouds or put it in a fortune cookie or horoscope or on a billboard?" God wants us to know that we don't need a horoscope, a psychic, or a palm reader to make the critical decisions in our lives. What are we to do? We're to make God our delight. When we do, we'll have the freedom to chase after our dreams—the ones He's placed in our hearts.

What does delighting in God give us the freedom to do?

There are two dangers associated with this principle. The first one is that we'll pursue our passions without making God our delight. Some may say, "I've got passions and I'm going to pursue them, that's all I needed to hear." We need to remember that there's an "a" part of the equation—the condition. Some people want to just focus on the "b" part of the equation—the desires. When we delight ourselves in the Lord, we won't care what other desires He puts in our hearts. Delighting ourselves in God puts us in a free position, because it places us at the point where we let go of our lives. We can't delight in the Lord when we hold onto our lives and elevate ourselves. We can't delight in the Lord when we're afraid to trust Him and still put our confidence in this world. The second danger is that we'll unwisely pursue the passions in us. Where do we get good advice to wisely pursue our passions? In future sessions we'll study how to gain wisdom by acting on the desires that God places in our hearts.

What are two dangers associated with pursuing the passions in our hearts?

So, what happens when our desires aren't met in our timing? Sometimes we have to go into "overtime" waiting for God to bring fulfillment to our passions. What keeps a team going when the game goes into overtime? The love of the game! The passion to win! What keeps us going is our love for God and our delight in "who" He is. But, what do we do when we're passionately in love with and connecting with God and the fulfillment of our desires is delayed, according to our timing? That's what the rest of this passage addresses. In verse 5, David provides the first thing we're to do: "Commit your way to the Lord." In verse 7, he gives the second: "Be still before the Lord and wait patiently for him." The key principle David gives us is that we *must wait actively and act dependently.* Our culture says that waiting is an inactive thing and acting is an independent thing. In God's economy, waiting is not an inactive but an active process. What does David mean when he says to "wait patiently for him"? Waiting means to abide in God, to link our lives with Him and His purposes. It means that we rest in the assurance

What is the key principle David gives us for waiting on God? Describe what this principle means to you.

50

God is at work in our lives and His will is being done. To take this one step further, what does it mean to wait actively? First, we seek Him with all our hearts. In verse 4, David instructs us to "Delight yourself in the Lord."

We should fall in love with Him and walk with Him daily. Second, we should always do the right thing. In verse 3, David writes, "Trust in the Lord and do good." We're to keep on doing the right and honorable thing, that which is full of integrity in every area and detail of our lives. In Luke 16:10, Jesus said that if we are not faithful in the little things, then we can't be trusted in the larger tasks. Some people will just try to slide by in the present, waiting for the bigger and better opportunities to come along. Waiting on God doesn't mean that we take a spiritual nap. Waiting is an active process where we develop our character and prove our trustworthiness.

In verse 5, David tells us to, "Trust in him [God] and he will do this." Acting dependently means that we trust God as He provides the answers and fulfills the desires of our hearts. The great danger we always face is being vastly dependent on God when we need an answer and becoming amazingly independent when we get an answer. If He gives us the road map, we might try to take off down the road and leave Jesus standing on the sidewalk. God wants us to wait actively and, once we get an answer, to act dependently with the same attitude we had when we waited actively. We may get the answer, lose contact with God, and be right out of God's will again. We must allow God to accomplish His will in and through our lives. In 1 Thessalonians 5:24, Paul reminds us: "The one who calls you is faithful and he will do it."

4

notes:

Remain in groups of 6–8 people, in a horseshoe configuration.

In this small-group session, students will be applying the lessons of the text to their own lives through the following questions.

The students were asked (in the student book) to choose an answer for each question and explain why.

Learning from the Story (5-7 minutes)

1. In verse 4, why do you think David mentions "delight yourself in the Lord" before "the desires of your heart"? What difference does it make if one gets before the other in your life?

2. What is the most difficult part of waiting on God? What benefits have you experienced when you've waited on God?

3. When you see an injustice, which of the following responses is most likely your first reaction?

   ☐ be still before God and pray (v. 7)
   ☐ remind myself of God's ultimate justice (v. 6)
   ☐ worry and become anxious (vv. 7–8)
   ☐ get angry (v. 8)
   ☐ trust God and return evil with good (v. 3)
   ☐ other:_____

notes:

life change lessons (5-7 minutes)

If you truly want to make God the delight of your life, what specific things can you do? Here are some good actions to start with:

1. REPRIORITIZE YOUR LIFE PASSIONS. Make a list of all the people, pursuits, and activities in your life that you are passionate about. Once you've made this list, rank them in order as best you can, starting with the ones you are most passionate about. Then, ask yourself, "Do I receive greater joy out of this than my relationship with God? Do I delight in this more than spending time with God?" Allow your answers to help you reprioritize what is important to you in your life.

2. <u>BE FAITHFUL IN THE LITTLE THINGS</u> WHILE YOU WAIT FOR GREATER OPPORTUNITIES. While you are waiting for God to fulfill your deepest desires and aspirations, exhibit integrity in all the areas of your life. Remember, your faithfulness in the "small things" is a BIG DEAL to God! Learn to wait actively! What are some beneficial things you can do while you wait on God for "greater things"?

3. SHARE YOUR TESTIMONY OFTEN OF HOW GOD IS GIVING YOU THE DESIRES OF YOUR HEART. <u>This will be a constant reminder that God will work through you to fulfill your desires</u>. Make sure you give God the credit He deserves, instead of claiming the credit for yourself, regarding the fulfillment of your God-given desires.

notes:

4

Share with the class the following thoughts on how the lessons of this text might be applied today. The answers to the student book questions (provided in the margin) are underlined unless the question requires a personal answer.

Make a list of all the people, pursuits, and activities in your life that you are passionate about. Once you've made this list, rank them in order as best you can, starting with the ones you are most passionate about. Then, reprioritize them in light of making God the delight of your life.

What should you do while you wait on God for greater things?

What is the purpose of sharing your testimony of how God is giving you the desires of your heart?

♡ Caring Time   (15-20 minutes)

⟳ CARING TIME
Remain in groups
of 6–8 people, in
a horseshoe
configuration.

Hand out the Prayer/
Praise Report to the
entire group. Ask each
subgroup to pray for
the empty chair. Pray
specifically for God to
guide you to someone
to bring next week to
fill that chair.

After a sufficient
time of prayer in
subgroups, close in
a corporate prayer.
Say, "Next week
we will talk about:
'Choosing God's Will.' "

Remind participants
of the daily Scripture
readings and reflective
questions found on
page 56.

Close by taking time to pray for one another and for your own special concerns. Begin by praying for the kind of heart that delights in God more than anything else. Also, use the Prayer/Praise Report and pray for the concerns listed.

Conclude your prayer time by reading Psalm 34:8–14 together:
Taste and see that the Lord is good;
  blessed is the man who takes refuge in him.
Fear the Lord, you his saints,
  for those who fear him lack nothing.
The lions may grow weak and hungry,
  but those who seek the Lord lack no good thing.
Come, my children, listen to me;
  I will teach you the fear of the Lord.
Whoever of you loves life
  and desires to see many good days,
keep your tongue from evil
  and your lips from speaking lies.
Turn from evil and do good;
  seek peace and pursue it.

notes:

BIBLE STUDY NOTES

PSALM 37:3
faith

PSALM 37:4
delight in God

PSALM 37:5

PSALM 37:6

PSALM 37:7
God's timing

PSALM 37:8
God's goodness

Reference Notes

Use these notes to gain further understanding
of the text as you study on your own.

trust in the Lord. This is a deep reliance on the God who promises to punish the ungodly and reward the righteous.

the land. Many interpreters see Israel's promised land as a type of heaven (John 14:1–6).

enjoy safe pasture. God's people are often analogized as sheep, with Jesus as the Shepherd (John 10:27–29).

Men and women who delight in God desire only what will please God. The desires mentioned here are not casual wishes but rather innermost desires.

heart. This refers to the center of the human spirit that produces emotions, thought, motivations, courage, and action (see Prov. 4:23).

Commit your way. This, literally, means "to roll it over on" the Lord. God's people can place the weight of life upon the Lord (see Phil. 4:6–7).

noonday sun. No shade of reproach or sin will remain.

Be still ... wait patiently. To hush the spirit and to be silent before the Lord, knowing that God's timing is never wrong.

do not fret. God's goodness is more evident in how He works through our troubles and defeats than in the successes of the wicked.

4

notes:

¹ "The Pastor's Story File," *Autoillustrator* on *www.crosswalk.com*, 1987.

Session

5

Choosing God's Will

Prepare for the Session

	READINGS	REFLECTIVE QUESTIONS
Monday	Philippians 2:5	What attitudes do you currently hold that are not Christ like? What needs to change?
Tuesday	Philippians 2:6–7	Do you consider yourself a servant to your family? To your friends? To your neighbors?
Wednesday	Philippians 2:8	How committed are you to obedience?
Thursday	Philippians 2:9	How do you honor Christ in your everyday life?
Friday	Philippians 2:10	What does the reality that one day you'll meet Jesus face-to-face mean to you?
Saturday	Philippians 2:11	Is there a person, pursuit, or possession in your life that has more control of you than Christ?
Sunday	Philippians 2:11	When was the last time you told someone of your allegiance to Christ as Lord?

notes:

OUR GOALS FOR THIS SESSION ARE:

⋃ In groups of 6–8, gather people in a horseshoe configuration.

Make sure everyone has a name tag.

Take time to share information on class parties that are coming up as well as any relevant church events.

INTRODUCE THE ICEBREAKER ACTIVITY: The students have been given instructions in their books.

After the Icebreaker say something like, "Letting go of something secure is always difficult! Today we will be talking about letting go of our own will and choosing to follow God's will."

Hand out the Prayer/Praise Report. A sample copy is on pages 158-159. Have people write down prayer requests and praises. Then have the prayer coordinator collect the report and make copies for use during the Caring Time.

✝

BIBLE STUDY
- to understand how Jesus kept the will of His Father as the first priority of His life
- to learn the importance of surrendering our lives to the will of God
- to learn to value eternal treasures more than earthly gain

LIFE CHANGE
- to list two or three things in our lives that pose a threat to our allegiance to Christ
- to keep a journal this week of the difficult choices we make
- to pray that God would give us discerning hearts

 Icebreaker (10-15 minutes)

Letting Go. As children, it's hard to let go of those things that bring security and comfort. Which of the following things did you have the most difficult time giving up as a child?

- ☐ my first tooth
- ☐ a security blanket or toy that I cuddled with at night
- ☐ my bottle
- ☐ the shallow end of the pool
- ☐ fear of the dark
- ☐ my parent's hand on the first day of school
- ☐ the training wheels on my bicycle
- ☐ other:_____

5

notes:

**LEARNING FROM
THE BIBLE**

PHILIPPIANS 2:5–11

**Have a member of
the class, selected
ahead of time, read
the passage from
Philippians.**

Bible Study   (30-45 minutes)

The Scripture for this week:

⁵*Your attitude should be the same as that of Christ Jesus:*
⁶*Who, being in very nature God,*
    did not consider equality with God something to be grasped,
⁷*but made himself nothing,*
    taking the very nature of a servant,
    being made in human likeness.
⁸*And being found in appearance as a man,*
    he humbled himself
    and became obedient to death—even death on a cross!
⁹*Therefore God exalted him to the highest place*
    and gave him the name that is above every name,
¹⁰*that at the name of Jesus every knee should bow,*
    in heaven and on earth and under the earth,
¹¹*and every tongue confess that Jesus Christ is Lord,*
    to the glory of God the Father.

notes:

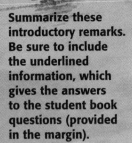

Summarize these introductory remarks. Be sure to include the underlined information, which gives the answers to the student book questions (provided in the margin).

...about today's session (5 minutes)

GETTING MOMENTUM ON YOUR SIDE

The more momentum is on your side, the less you have to struggle to make progress. If you decided to take your Bible study group on a white water rafting trip, you would start at an entry point somewhere upstream and paddle hard to make headway. As the river's current grows stronger and carries your boat downstream, your primary concern becomes steering rather than starting. Starting momentum takes more effort and more time. From the beginning of the trip when you put your raft in the water, you are allowing the current, the natural momentum of the water, to move your raft ever faster through the difficult rapids.

Like whitewater rafting, the decisions we make are easier and come with less struggle when momentum is on our side. How do we get momentum on our side? We decide to do the will of God from the start. What does *God's will* or *the will of God* mean? God's will is simply what God desires for us to do and become. We live every day in the "current" of God's will. Some believers wait until a difficult choice arises before deciding whether to fight the current (God's will) or "go with the flow." <u>Choices are much easier to make when we are committed from the beginning to doing God's will in all things</u>. Everything that helps fulfill God's purposes in the world, and in your life, is a "yes" and everything that doesn't is a "no." With this momentum on our side, we won't have to paddle against the stream and get discouraged. <u>God wants to carry us down the river and safely through life's rapids. All He wants is for us to let Him steer and maneuver through the rapids with His power behind us</u>. Life is much easier that way. Today's session will examine several principles from Jesus' life on this earth that will help us live in the will of God and be wise in our decision making.

According to the leader, what makes choices easier to make?

Describe how the leader compared white water rafting to surrendering to the will of God.

5

notes:

⛇ Remain in groups of 6–8 people, in a horseshoe configuration.

In this small group session, students will be responding to the following questions that will help them share their stories in terms of the words of Paul regarding the obedience of Jesus to the will of God in Philippians 2:5–11.

Have the students explore these questions together.

Identifying with the Story (5-7 minutes)

1. Which one of the following most accurately describes your first thoughts when you hear the word *servant*?

   ☐ butler or maid   ☐ hired help
   ☐ slave   ☐ humble
   ☐ hard worker   ☐ low status
   ☐ underprivileged   ☐ leader
   ☐ loving   ☐ other:_____

2. What do you think was the most difficult part of Jesus' earthly life when He became a human?

   ☐ getting physically tired and weak
   ☐ not being recognized as the Son of God by the people He had given life
   ☐ training 12 disciples to change the world
   ☐ knowing that His life would end up on a cruel cross
   ☐ dealing with the religious leaders
   ☐ resisting temptation
   ☐ not flaunting His supernatural power
   ☐ other:_____

3. At what times in your life do you have the greatest difficulty being a servant and why?

notes:

today's session (15-20 minutes)

Share with your class the following information which you may modify according to your own perspectives and teaching needs. The answers to the student book questions (provided in the margin) are underlined.

Coming up with answers to life's difficult questions can be overwhelming. As believers, we can be encouraged that Jesus is with us and ready to give the insight and help we need. If our commitment is to live in the will of God, Jesus will be there to help us in the critical decisions of life including relationships, finances, careers, and ministry. In Matthew 10:19–20, Jesus knew His disciples would encounter difficult situations and, therefore, encouraged them with these words: " 'But when they arrest you, do not worry about what to say or how to say it. At that time you will be given what to say, for it will not be you speaking, but the Spirit of your Father speaking through you.' " God is there to give us wisdom when words seem to fail us. Here's a story that illustrates this point:

> A famous scientist was on his way to give another lecture when his chauffeur offered an idea. "Hey, boss, I've heard your speech so many times, I bet I could deliver it and give you the night off."
>
> "Sounds great," the scientist said.
>
> When they got to the auditorium, the scientist put on the chauffeur's hat and settled into the back row. The chauffeur walked to the lectern and delivered the speech. Afterward he asked if there were any questions.
>
> "Yes," said one professor. Then he launched into a highly technical question.
>
> The chauffeur was panic-stricken for a moment but quickly recovered. "That's an easy one," he replied. "So easy, I'm going to let my chauffeur answer it."[1]

5

There are also times in our lives when we face circumstances that leave us struggling with knowing how to pray. In Romans 8:26, Paul gives us these encouraging words: "In the same way, the Spirit helps us in our weakness. We do not know what we ought to pray for, but the Spirit himself intercedes for us with groans that words cannot express." We can draw encouragement from the fact that God is eager to help us know what to <u>say</u> and what to <u>pray</u>. But there's one condition. <u>We must be committed to following God's will.</u> If we waffle on this point, we will be like the person that James describes in James 1:6–8: "When he asks, he must believe and not doubt, because he who doubts is like a wave of the sea, blown and tossed by the wind. That man should not think he will receive anything from the Lord; he is a double-minded man, unstable in all he does." Today's session will give us insight into how Jesus was so consistent in His commitment to living in His Father's will. We'll look at His life and the choices He made, and draw out some principles for our lives.

God is eager to help us know what to _____ and what to _____.

What condition does God want us to meet in order for us to get this help?

today's session (cont'd)

Jesus Intended to Do the Will of God From the Start

Jesus was intentional. No one "just happens" to do the will of God in his or her life. We live in God's will when we are intentional in our choices and our choices are controlled by our desire to live within His plan. In verse 5, Paul tells us that, "Your attitude should be the same as that of Christ Jesus." In other words, we should think like Christ and live like Christ. In verse 7, we gain insight into what this means for us: "[Jesus] made himself nothing, taking the very nature of a servant, being made in human likeness." Jesus made a choice to lay aside His incomparable power and take on humanity. In doing so, He modeled for us how to be a servant who willingly serves the Father. In verses 8–11, Paul paints a vivid picture of someone who did His Father's will intentionally from the beginning. We see in verse 8 that from day one Jesus knew what He was about to do: "And being found in appearance as a man, he humbled himself and became obedient to death—even death on a cross!" Jesus let go of His life as the Son of God and surrendered it to the current of the will of God. In John 6:38, Jesus said, " 'For I have come down from heaven not to do my will but to do the will of him who sent me.' " God is not asking to negotiate with us, but rather for us to surrender to the flow of His purposes in this life. Many people may say, "I don't need you to tell me how to live, I just need a little help." God, however, is asking us to surrender, to completely abandon our own agendas, and follow Jesus' agenda for us.

What do verses 8–11 reveal about Jesus' intention regarding His life on earth?

Jesus Surrendered Day-by-Day

What three examples did the leader give that demonstrated Jesus' commitment to the will of His Father?

Let's look at three instances in Jesus' life that demonstrate the way "he humbled himself and become obedient to death—even death on a cross!" (v. 8). In the first situation, we find Jesus in the aftermath of an amazing miracle where He had just fed 5,000 families with a boy's lunch. The people were so impressed that they wanted to make Jesus their earthly king! Here's Jesus' response in John 6:15: "Jesus, knowing that they intended to come and make him king by force, withdrew again to a mountain by himself." Jesus chose to resist this offer of power by removing Himself from the situation because He didn't come for earthly power gained through political means. Jesus knew that following God's will for His life would accomplish greater things.

John 6:15:

_____

In the second situation, we find one of His closest friends rebuking Him for the thought of going to the cross to die. Let's see how Jesus responded in Mark 8:33: "When Jesus turned and looked at his disciples, he rebuked Peter. 'Get behind me, Satan!' he said. 'You do not have in mind the things of God, but the things of men.' " Again, Jesus was faced with the tension between His human nature which longed for survival and safety and God's will. Jesus knew that the things of God were more important than the things of men.

Mark 8:33:

In the third situation, we find Jesus in the Garden of Gethsemane, struggling with the idea of facing death on the cross. Jesus faced this conflict of agony or physical safety and well-being and made the decision to follow God's will. In Matthew 26:42, Jesus prayed, " 'My Father, if it is not possible for this cup to be taken away unless I drink it, may your will be done.' " These are only three of many instances where Jesus surrendered to His Father's will.

Matthew 26:42

He Knew What True Treasure Was

If we commit our lives to following God's will, we run the risk of being misunderstood and missing out on some worldly pleasures and material gain. There is great difficulty in trying to live within the current of God's will and purposes unless the thought of eternity dominates our minds. We must realize that there's more to life than this life. In John 6:39–40, Jesus proves that He had us and eternity on His mind: " 'This is the will of him who sent me, that I shall lose none of all that he has given me, but raise them up at the last day. For my Father's will is that everyone who looks to the Son and believes in him shall have eternal life, and I will raise him up at the last day.' "

What risks are associated with surrendering to the will of God in our lives?

What should dominate our minds as we try to live out God's will and purposes?

5

Jesus willingly bypassed what He could gain on this earth for our sake. All along the way, Jesus was conscious of the heavenly prize before Him that would last for eternity. We see this in Hebrews 12:2: "Let us fix our eyes on Jesus, the author and perfecter of our faith, who for the joy set before him endured the cross, scorning its shame, and sat down at the right hand of the throne of God." Jesus knew that what He "lost" in terms of earth, He would gain in terms of heaven. When we decide from the start that our lives are committed to living in the will of God, great momentum is on our side for making wise decisions and gaining eternal rewards.

notes:

✝

Remain in groups of 6–8 people, in a horseshoe configuration.

In this small-group session, students will be applying the lessons of the text to their own lives through the following questions.

The students were asked (in the student book) to choose an answer for each question and explain why.

Learning from the Story (5-7 minutes)

1. Which of the following statements from our Scripture passage would be the most difficult for you to follow if you were in Jesus' shoes? Which would be the easiest for you to follow?

   ☐ "did not consider equality with God something to be grasped" (v. 6)
   ☐ "made himself nothing" (v. 7)
   ☐ "taking the very nature of a servant" (v. 7)
   ☐ "being made in human likeness" (v. 7)
   ☐ "he humbled himself" (v. 8)
   ☐ "became obedient to death—even death on a cross!" (v. 8)

2. What person in your life would you consider a servant? What qualities does he or she display that you admire?

3. If this group interviewed someone very close to you and asked them to complete the following statement about you, how do you think that person would answer? "_____ (your name) is a servant in the way he/she ..."

notes:

life change lessons (5-7 minutes)

Share with the class the following thoughts on how the lessons of this text might be applied today. The answers to the student book questions (provided in the margin) are underlined unless the question requires a personal answer.

What is the greatest threat you face in letting God have complete control of your life?

What difficult choices do you expect to face this week? What truths have you learned from this session that will help you make the right choices?

Making the right choices in life is much easier when you've unwaveringly concluded who has your allegiance. How can you stay committed to living in the will of God each day of your life? Here are three steps to help you get started:

1. LIST TWO OR THREE THINGS IN YOUR LIFE THAT POSE A THREAT TO YOUR ALLEGIANCE TO CHRIST. Jesus faced all kinds of obstacles to His mission to accomplish God's will. What are the top two or three areas of your life that compete for your attention and allegiance to Christ? Identify these obstacles and ask someone to keep you accountable in those areas.

2. KEEP A JOURNAL THIS WEEK OF THE DIFFICULT CHOICES YOU MAKE. Each day you are faced with many choices that you don't think twice about, such as what to wear and your route to work. You will, however, face choices this week that challenge your commitment to live in the will of God.

These choices may deal with areas such as how you handle your money, how you treat people, your fleshly desires, what you watch with your eyes, etc. At the end of each day, list the critical choices you made that day and ask yourself whether you responded in a way that proved your obedience to Scripture and your allegiance to God's expectations of you.

3. PRAY THAT GOD WILL GIVE YOU A DISCERNING HEART. As you cast yourself into the current of God's will, you will need wisdom and courage to maneuver through the rapids. As you surrender to the current and flow of God's will in your life, He will carry you in the right direction. As you face difficult decisions, you need a discerning heart that is able to hear God's direction as He guides you through the dips and turns in the river of life.

notes:

Caring Time   (15-20 minutes)

Remember that this time is for developing and expressing your care for each other by sharing any personal prayer requests and praying for each other's needs. Pray for the group member to your right that he or she will commit to following God's will and remembering daily the eternal rewards that are awaiting each Christian. Also, use the Prayer/Praise Report and pray for the concerns listed.

 notes:

Reference Notes

Use these notes to gain further understanding
of the text as you study on your own.

There is little agreement between scholars as to how this hymn breaks into verses or how it is to be phrased. However, one thing is clear. The hymn has two equal parts. Part one (vv. 6–8) focuses on the self-humiliation of Jesus. Part two (vv. 9–11) focuses on God's exaltation of Jesus. In part one, Jesus is the subject of the two main verbs, while in part two God is the subject of the two main verbs.

being. This is not the normal Greek word for "being." This word carries the idea of preexistence. By using it, Paul is saying Jesus always existed in the form of God.

very nature. The Greek word is *morphe* (used twice by Paul in this hymn). He says Jesus was "in very nature God," and He then took upon Himself "the very nature of a servant." This is a key word in understanding the nature of Christ.

to be grasped. This is a rare word, used only at this point in the New Testament. It refers to the fact that Jesus did not have to "snatch" equality with God. Equality was not something He needed to acquire. It was His already, and He could give it away. Giving, not grasping, is what Jesus did.

CARING TIME
Remain in groups of 6–8 people, in a horseshoe configuration.

Hand out the Prayer/Praise Report to the entire group. Ask each subgroup to pray for the empty chair. Pray specifically for God to guide you to someone to bring next week to fill that chair.

After a sufficient time of prayer in subgroups, close in a corporate prayer. Say, "Next week we will talk about: 'Choosing God's Forgiveness.'"

BIBLE STUDY NOTES

PHILIPPIANS 2:6–11
Christ's humility

PHILIPPIANS 2:6
equality with God

PHILIPPIANS 2:7
slavehood

made himself nothing. Literally, "to empty," or "to pour out until the container is empty."

taking the very nature of a servant. Jesus gave up Godhood and took on slavehood. From being the ultimate master, He became the lowest servant. He left ruling for serving.

being made. In contrast to the verb in verse 6 (that stresses Christ's eternal nature), this verb points to the fact that at a particular time He was born in the likeness of a human being.

human likeness. Jesus did not just seem to be human. He assumed the identity and flesh of a human being and was similar in all ways to other human beings.

PHILIPPIANS 2:8
obedience

in appearance as a man. The word translated "in appearance" is *schema* and denotes that which is outward and changeable (distinct from *morphe*, which denotes that which is essential and eternal).

he humbled himself. This is the central point of one who lived a life of self-sacrifice, self-renunciation, and self-surrender.

obedient to death. The extent of this humbling is defined by this clause. Jesus humbled Himself to the furthest point one can go. He submitted to death itself for the sake of both God and humanity. There was not a more dramatic way to demonstrate humility.

death on a cross. This was no ordinary death. Crucifixion was a harsh, demeaning, and utterly painful way to die. According to the Old Testament, those who died by hanging on a tree were considered to have been cursed by God.

PHILIPPIANS 2:9
character

name. In the ancient world, a name was more than just a way of distinguishing one individual from another. It revealed the inner nature or character of a person. The name given the resurrected Jesus is the supreme name—the name above all names—because this is Jesus' identity in His innermost being.

PHILIPPIANS 2:10

bow. Everyone will one day pay homage to Jesus. This worship will come from all of creation—all angels (in heaven), all people (on earth), and all demons (under the earth).

PHILIPPIANS 2:11

Jesus Christ is Lord. The climax of this hymn. This is the earliest and most basic confession of faith on the part of the church (see Acts 2:36; Rom. 10:9; 1 Cor. 12:3).

Lord. This is the name that was given to Jesus; the name that reflects who He really is (see v. 9). This is the name of God. Jesus is the supreme Sovereign of the universe.

5

notes:

[1] *Reader's Digest*, April 1998, 71.

Session

6

Choosing God's Forgiveness

Prepare for the Session

	READINGS	REFLECTIVE QUESTIONS
Monday	Hebrews 12:1	What in your life is hindering you from following Christ in obedience?
Tuesday	Hebrews 12:2	Would you say that your eyes are fixed on Jesus or on something else?
Wednesday	Hebrews 12:3	What causes you to "grow weary and lose heart" the most in your life?
Thursday	Hebrews 12:4	What is the temptation you struggle with the most?
Friday	Hebrews 12:5–8	Can you point to a time in your life when the Lord exercised discipline? What was the result?
Saturday	Hebrews 12:9–10	In what area of your life would you like to reflect more of God's holiness?
Sunday	Hebrews 12:11	Why is it easier to recognize God's discipline in your life once it's completed its work rather than in the midst of it?

notes:

OUR GOALS FOR
THIS SESSION ARE:

⚘ In groups of 6–8, gather people in a horseshoe configuration.

Make sure everyone has a name tag.

Take time to share information on class parties that are coming up as well as any relevant church events.

INTRODUCE THE ICEBREAKER ACTIVITY: The students have been given instructions in their books.

After the Icebreaker say something like, "A team effort and the support of other Christians can help us remain faithful to God in the events of life. But, unfortunately, there are times we all make poor choices. Today, we will talk about how God's discipline and forgiveness can get us back on track."

Hand out the Prayer/Praise Report. A sample copy is on pages 158-159. Have people write down prayer requests and praises. Then have the prayer coordinator collect the report and make copies for use during the Caring Time.

BIBLE STUDY
- to understand that our sinful choices have consequences
- to know how God responds to us when we sin
- to know how we should respond to God when we sin

LIFE CHANGE
- to confess to God any unconfessed sin in our lives
- to accept God's forgiveness for the sins we've committed in our lives this week
- to ask someone we trust to partner with us in prayer concerning the sin that gives us the most trouble

Icebreaker   (10-15 minutes)

Track Team. Your group is forming a track team. The next track meet has six events that your members can enter. Decide which one of these races you would enter each of your group members in based on the time you've spent together.

- ☐ 100 Meter Dash—The one who exhibits great bursts of energy and joy.
- ☐ Marathon—The one who is steady and dependable.
- ☐ 4 x 400 Relay—The one who is a real team player and gets along well with others.
- ☐ 100 Meter Hurdles—The one who has strong faith that helps him or her hurdle obstacles in life.
- ☐ Long Jump—The one who is eager to jump right in and help get tasks completed on time.
- ☐ High Jump—The one who exhibits a high level of encouragement to the people around him or her.

6

notes:

LEARNING FROM THE BIBLE

HEBREWS 12:1–11

Select two members of the class to read the passage from Hebrews. Have one member read verses 1–6, and the other read verses 7–11.

Bible Study   (30-45 minutes)

The Scripture for this week:

¹*Since we are surrounded by such a great cloud of witnesses, let us throw off everything that hinders and the sin that so easily entangles, and let us run with perseverance the race marked out for us.* ²*Let us fix our eyes on Jesus, the author and perfecter of our faith, who for the joy set before him endured the cross, scorning its shame, and sat down at the right hand of the throne of God.* ³*Consider him who endured such opposition from sinful men, so that you will not grow weary and lose heart.*

⁴*In your struggle against sin, you have not yet resisted to the point of shedding your blood.* ⁵*And you have forgotten that word of encouragement that addresses you as sons:*

"*My son, do not make light of the Lord's discipline,*

and do not lose heart when he rebukes you,

⁶*because the Lord disciplines those he loves,*

and he punishes everyone he accepts as a son."

⁷*Endure hardship as discipline; God is treating you as sons. For what son is not disciplined by his father?* ⁸*If you are not disciplined (and everyone undergoes discipline), then you are illegitimate children and not true sons.* ⁹*Moreover, we have all had human fathers who disciplined us and we respected them for it. How much more should we submit to the Father of our spirits and live!* ¹⁰*Our fathers disciplined us for a little while as they thought best; but God disciplines us for our good, that we may share in his holiness.* ¹¹*No discipline seems pleasant at the time, but painful. Later on, however, it produces a harvest of righteousness and peace for those who have been trained by it.*

notes:

Summarize these introductory remarks. Be sure to include the underlined information, which gives the answers to the student book questions (provided in the margin).

...about today's session (5 minutes)

MAKING UP FOR COSTLY PENALTIES

Football coaches hate penalties on their team. Just when they are making progress against their opponent, their team is penalized for rules violations such as holding, offsides, illegal motion, pass interference, face-masking, and personal foul. It's a helpless feeling for the coach as the referee takes the ball and marks off yardage in the direction of the opposing team. Great teams work to reduce penalties. Great teams also work together and make up lost yardage.

What two things do great teams do regarding penalties?

In today's session, we'll look at our response, as well as God's response, to the disobedience in our lives. What should we expect from God after we make sinful choices? Some people think He treats us like the seagull in the following story:

A daddy was at the beach with his children when his four-year-old son ran up to him, grabbed his hand, and led him to a place in the sand where a seagull lay dead. "Daddy, what happened to him?" the son asked. "He died and went to heaven," the dad replied. The boy thought a moment and then said, "Did God throw him back down?"

In the story of the seagull, in what way does the son's view of God parallel many Christians' view of God?

Today we'll look at Hebrews 12:1–11 and see God's actions and attitudes toward His children when they break the rules.

6

notes:

✝

♘ **Remain in groups of 6–8 people, in a horseshoe configuration.**

In this small group session, students will be responding to the following questions that will help them share their stories in terms of God's discipline as discussed in Hebrews 12:1–11.

Have the students explore these questions together.

Identifying with the Story (5-7 minutes)

1. When you were a teenager, what action or attitude most often resulted in being disciplined by your parents?

   ☐ coming home late   ☐ talking back
   ☐ getting bad grades   ☐ skipping school
   ☐ hanging around with the wrong people
   ☐ other:_____

2. Do you think you deserved the discipline you received as a child?

3. The writer of Hebrews describes the Christian life as a race. What kind of race most accurately describes your Christian life?

   ☐ **Stock Car Race**—mostly traveling around in circles at a fast pace
   ☐ **Drag Race**—fast-paced, short spurts with a lot of excitement
   ☐ **Motocross Racing**—lots of ups, downs, and turns
   ☐ **Demolition Derby**—lots of damage, not to mention near misses
   ☐ **Go-cart Racing**—still doing too many immature things
   ☐ **Yacht Racing**—relying on the Spirit's wind in my sails to help me navigate through the waves and storms
   ☐ other:_____

4. Have you ever experienced God's discipline? If so, what has been the greatest lesson you've learned as a result of God's discipline in your life? Was it pleasant as you went through it? How are you different now?

notes:

today's session (15-20 minutes)

Share with your class the following information which you may modify according to your own perspectives and teaching needs. The answers to the student book questions (provided in the margin) are underlined.

How does the way we respond to failure affect our lives?

How did the leader describe sin?

What do the following verses tell us about the outcome of sin?

• *Romans 6:23*

• *Galatians 6:7*

This Bible study series focuses on the critical decisions we face every day. Most of the sessions deal with how to make wise choices. This session, however, deals with our poor choices. How we handle failure has a tremendous impact on our lives. What we do when we fail says a great deal about our character. Handling failure is much more difficult than handling success.

Let's look at what the Bible says about the greatest failure in our lives: sin. Sin means that we miss the mark of God's righteousness and holiness with the choices we make. The nature of sin is that it always leads to death. In Romans 6:23, Paul writes, "For the wages of sin is death, but the gift of God is eternal life in Christ Jesus our Lord." Before we place our faith in Christ, our spirit is dead because of sin. This means that we're separated from God and are in a broken relationship with Him. Sin also leads to the death of things in our lives such as relationships, dreams, reputation, and joy. All sin has consequences. Someone once said that sooner or later we will all sit down to a banquet of consequences. In Galatians 6:7, we read, "Do not be deceived: God cannot be mocked. A man reaps what he sows."

In football, teams that are penalized lose 5 to 15 yards depending on the severity of the infraction. When we sin, we incur consequences in our lives. What those consequences are depends on the sin and the situation. When we run away from God's direction in our lives and make our own choices, we'll have to face the consequences. Roy Riegels discovered what it means to run the wrong direction and face the consequences.

Football's "Wrongest Run" occurred in the 1929 Rose Bowl. California was leading Georgia Tech 7–6 when Roy Riegels took the ball. He became confused when his California teammates began blocking Tech men behind the ball. He turned and ran in that direction.

The crowd roared in amazement. "Wrong way! Wrong way!" Benny Lom, a fast California halfback, started after Riegels who was headed straight for the opponent's goal. "Roy, Roy, stop!" he cried.

But the noise was so great that Riegels thought the crowd was cheering him on. Just as he reached the goal, his teammate pulled him down.

The California team tried to punt from their one-yard line. But Tech blocked the kick and pounced on the ball behind the goal. The play was scored as a two-point safety for Georgia Tech. This proved to be Georgia Tech's margin of victory.

6

today's session (cont'd)

Surely Riegels' fans, teammates, and coaches were disappointed at the wrong-way run and the outcome of the game. But, what happens when we run the wrong way as Christians? Let's look at God's response to our sin, and then take a look at what our response should be.

God's Response

According to 1 John 2:1 and Hebrews 12:1, what does God desire in the lives of His children?

In 1 John 2 we get a glimpse of God's response to sin in the lives of His children. In verse 1, the apostle John writes, "My dear children, I write this to you so that you will not sin." God's desire for us is that we avoid sin, not only because of how it can wreck our lives but because of how it casts a shadow on the ability of others to see His glory (see Matt. 5:16). In Hebrews 12:1, this writer also urges God's children to "throw off everything that hinders and the sin that so easily entangles." God's desire for us is that we do not sin.

So, what is God's response when Christians do sin? John gives us the answer in the second part of 1 John 2:1: "But if anybody does sin, we have one who speaks to the Father in our defense—Jesus Christ, the Righteous One." God's response to us is one of love as He recognizes the faith we've placed in His Son, the One who gave His life so we wouldn't have to. Sometimes we have a hard time understanding this truth. In Romans 8:38–39, Paul wanted to make this truth clear to us: "For I am convinced that neither death nor life, neither angels nor demons, neither the present nor the future, nor any powers, neither height nor depth, nor anything else in all creation, will be able to separate us from the love of God that is in Christ Jesus our Lord."

Describe the way Hebrews 12:7–10 compares an earthly father's discipline to that of our heavenly Father. What's similar? What's different?

The writer of Hebrews shows us that part of God's love is displayed in the way He disciplines His children. In verses 7–10, God's discipline is compared to that of a father who disciplines his children out of love. In verse 9, the writer says, "We have all had human fathers who disciplined us and we respected them for it." The purpose of God's discipline in our lives is that we become more like Christ: "God disciplines us for our good, that we may share in his holiness" (v. 10). Experiencing God's discipline is not pleasant when we experience it, but later on, "produces a harvest of righteousness and peace for those who have been trained by it" (v. 11). If your child ran out into the street without looking, you might discipline your child out of love and concern for his or her well being. In the same way, God wants us to understand the harm that sin inevitably brings into our lives.

God uses all of our experiences and turns them into growth opportunities. In Romans 8:28, Paul writes, "We know that in all things God works for the good of those who love him, who have been called according to his purpose." God takes all things, whether good or bad, and works them for His purposes. God never wastes an experience.

Sometimes we respond to the Spirit's conviction in our hearts about our sin and turn from our sinful attitudes and actions. Sometimes discipline is required. Either way, God desires that our hearts are humbled and headed for Him. In Psalm 51:17, we see the kind of heart that God desires in his children: "The sacrifices of God are a broken spirit; <u>a broken and contrite heart</u>, O God, you will not despise." God's desire is to restore us gently into a right relationship with Him. In Galatians 6:1, Paul encourages us to do this with our fellow Christians: "Brothers, if someone is caught in a sin, you who are spiritual should restore him gently."

According to Psalm 51:17, what kind of heart does God desire in His children?

Our Response

In Hebrews 12, let's look at how we are to respond to the realization of sin in our lives. In verse 1, we are encouraged to take whatever habit or temptation we are most prone to give in to and give it up: "Let us throw off everything that hinders and the sin that so easily entangles." In these verses, the image is one of someone running in a race. The fastest runners are those who have taken off robes or other garments in order to free the movement of their arms and legs. God knows that sin will hinder our walk and effectiveness for Him.

Our next response is to fix our eyes on Jesus, looking to Him for strength and encouragement. Hebrews 12:1–2 contains the two parts of repentance. <u>First, we're to stop our current sinful behavior and turn from it, seeing our sin the way God sees it, as disobedience. Then, we should turn to God and trust in His love and promises</u>. As we run in God's race, we should make sure we intentionally surround ourselves with "witnesses" who walk with Christ and are willing to encourage us and hold us accountable for the decisions that we make. Then, all of us can "run with perseverance the race marked out for us" (Heb. 12:1).

What are the two parts of repentance mentioned in Hebrews 12:1–2?

6

notes:

⊕

🧲 Remain in groups of 6–8 people, in a horseshoe configuration.

In this small-group session, students will be applying the lessons of the text to their own lives through the following questions.

The students were asked (in the student book) to choose an answer for each question and explain why.

Learning from the Story (5-7 minutes)

1. Which people in your life need the encouragement of someone cheering them on as they run the race that God has given them?

2. When was the last time you shared with someone a struggle or temptation you were having a hard time dealing with? What was the result of your honesty?

3. What has helped you keep your eyes fixed on Jesus?
   ☐ reading Scripture on a regular basis
   ☐ praying on a regular basis
   ☐ resting in God's forgiveness instead of trying to earn it
   ☐ studying the Bible with other believers
   ☐ sharing Christ with non-Christians
   ☐ using my spiritual gifts
   ☐ other:_____

notes:

life change lessons (5-7 minutes)

Share with the class the following thoughts on how the lessons of this text might be applied today. The answers to the student book questions (provided in the margin) are underlined unless the question requires a personal answer.

What does Romans 8:1 say about those who are Christians?

What are three ways you can respond to a loving God when you sin?

Many Christians think God gets angry or disgusted with them when they sin. <u>But Paul tells us in Romans 8:1, "There is now no condemnation for those who are in Christ Jesus."</u> Yes, God does grieve as a result of our sin, but His love for us remains the same because we're "in Christ." What are some practical steps we can take in responding to a loving God when we sin? Here are three:

1. <u>CONFESS TO GOD ANY UNCONFESSED SIN IN YOUR LIFE</u>. God wants you to realize the harm sin causes to your ability to communicate with Him and fulfill His purposes in your life. The first step is to understand God's heart toward the sins you commit. You need to trust His promises for your life more than the false hope that sin holds out. An example of confession is found in Psalm 51:3–4, as David confessed his sin of adultery with Bathsheba: "For I know my transgressions, and my sin is always before me. Against you, you only, have I sinned and done what is evil in your sight."

2. <u>ACCEPT GOD'S FORGIVENESS FOR THE SINS YOU'VE COMMITTED IN YOUR LIFE THIS WEEK</u>. Think about the sins you've committed this past week. Have you accepted the fact that God has already completely forgiven you of those sins? First John 1:9 says, "If we confess our sins, he is faithful and just and will forgive us our sins and purify us from all unrighteousness."

3. <u>ASK SOMEONE YOU TRUST TO PARTNER WITH YOU IN PRAYER CONCERNING THE SIN THAT GIVES YOU THE MOST TROUBLE</u>. As Hebrews 12:1 says, we're to do everything we can to rid our lives of the sin that so easily trips us up. Many Christians try to combat these areas alone. James 5:16 says, "Confess your sins to each other and pray for each other." We need the strength and encouragement of one another. Hebrews 10:24 encourages us to "consider how we may spur one another on toward love and good deeds."

6

notes:

CARING TIME
Remain in groups of 6–8 people, in a horseshoe configuration.

Hand out the Prayer/Praise Report to the entire group. Ask each subgroup to pray for the empty chair. Pray specifically for God to guide you to someone to bring next week to fill that chair.

After a sufficient time of prayer in subgroups, close in a corporate prayer. Say, "Next week we will talk about: 'Choosing God's Authority.' "

Caring Time (15-20 minutes)

Remember that this time is for developing and expressing your care for each other by sharing any personal prayer requests and praying for each other's needs. Pray for the group member to your right that he or she will commit to following God's will and remembering daily the eternal rewards that are awaiting each Christian. Also, use the Pray and Praise pages and pray for the concerns listed.

notes:

BIBLE STUDY NOTES

Reference Notes

Use these notes to gain further understanding of the text as you study on your own.

HEBREWS 2:1
heroes of faith

witnesses. This is the same word as the one for "martyrs." It is probably a deliberate play on words in which both meanings are intended. The heroes of faith are pictured as a cheering section of former runners, urging contemporary runners to keep on as they did.
throw off everything. In Greek games at the time, runners ran naked so that no clothes would hinder their movement.
the sin that so easily entangles. Just as a flowing robe makes it impossible to run, so sin prevents one from pursuing Christ.

HEBREWS 12:2
the prize

fix our eyes on Jesus. In races of the time, the prize for the race was placed at the end to motivate the runners. Jesus is here described as the prize upon which we are to focus.
joy set before him. Jesus knew the joy His mission of reconciliation would bring, and so pursued it whatever the cost. The readers are to follow that model.
scorning its shame. Crucifixion was considered so degrading that no Roman citizen could be crucified regardless of the crime committed.

HEBREWS 12:3
faithful living

Consider him. Instead of seeing opposition as an excuse to abandon faith, they should look to Jesus as a model of how to live faithfully through it.
weary and lose heart. These words were used in athletic circles to describe the collapse of a runner.

HEBREWS 12:4

shedding your blood. The persecution they have experienced so far has not yet included the ultimate sacrifice made by Jesus.

HEBREWS 12:5–6

A quote from Proverbs 3:11–12 (from the Septuagint), used to substantiate the author's point.

HEBREWS 12:7–11
discipline

At this time, corporal punishment of children was seen as a sign of a father's concern that his children learn right from wrong. Although children whose parents do not train or restrict them in any way seem to have more freedom, it is the children whose parents love them enough to administer discipline that grow into mature, responsible adults. In the same way, hardship is seen as a sign of God's care, since such discipline leads to growth in righteousness and peace.

notes:

6

Session

7

Choosing God's Authority

Prepare for the Session

	READINGS	REFLECTIVE QUESTIONS
Monday	Genesis 2:15	What responsibilities did God give Adam? Are you being a good steward with what God has given you?
Tuesday	Genesis 2:16–17	How much freedom did God give Adam in the garden? What one thing did God instruct Adam not to do and what was the consequence of disobeying Him?
Wednesday	Genesis 3:1	What question did the serpent ask the woman? Why does Satan want us to question what God has said?
Thursday	Genesis 3:2–3	Did the woman understand what God had said? Do you understand the consequences of disobeying God?
Friday	Genesis 3:4	Why does Satan want you to downplay the consequences of disobeying God?
Saturday	Genesis 3:5	Why does Satan want you to question God's motives?
Sunday	Genesis 3:6	What choice did the woman make and what were her reasons? Was it worth it?

notes:

7

OUR GOALS FOR THIS SESSION ARE:	

OUR GOALS FOR THIS SESSION ARE:

🔔 In groups of 6–8, gather people in a horseshoe configuration.

Make sure everyone has a name tag.

Take time to share information on class parties that are coming up as well as any relevant church events.

INTRODUCE THE ICEBREAKER ACTIVITY: The students have been given instructions in their books.

After the Icebreaker say something like, "We all grow up and live under someone else's authority. In today's session, we will explore the importance of accepting God's authority in our lives. We will see how doing so results in freedom rather than restriction."

Hand out the Prayer/Praise Report. A sample copy is on pages 158-159. Have people write down prayer requests and praises. Then have the prayer coordinator collect the report and make copies for use during the Caring Time.

BIBLE STUDY
- to understand the consequences of making choices apart from God's authority
- to learn that maximum freedom in life is a result of placing our lives under God's authority
- to understand that rules, apart from a relationship with God, lead to a lack of trust and rebellion

LIFE CHANGE
- to make a list of the pros and cons of being under someone else's authority
- to make a list of God's commands in Scripture that we find the most difficult to follow and ask God to give us a willingness to obey them
- to invest in a daily time with God, getting to know Him better

Icebreaker (10-15 minutes)

Authority Figures. Our society is filled with all types of authority figures. Which one of the following reminds you the most of yourself?

☐ POLICE OFFICER—I work to keep law and order among those around me.

☐ POLITICIAN—I try to put a positive spin on everything.

☐ PARENT—I enjoy looking out for the welfare of others.

☐ PROFESSOR—I strive to help others learn as much as they can.

☐ PASTOR—I enjoy being a spiritual leader and protector of people.

☐ PARTY PLANNER—I enjoy entertaining others and making sure they are having a good time.

notes:

**LEARNING FROM
THE BIBLE**

GENESIS 2:15–17

3:1–6

**Select four people
from your class
ahead of time to
read the passages
from Genesis. Have
one person be the
narrator, another
read the words of
God, another the
serpent, and the
fourth person the
words of Eve.**

Bible Study (30-45 minutes)

The Scripture for this week:

¹⁵*The Lord God took the man and put him in the Garden of Eden to work it and take care of it.* ¹⁶*And the Lord God commanded the man, "You are free to eat from any tree in the garden;* ¹⁷*but you must not eat from the tree of the knowledge of good and evil, for when you eat of it you will surely die."*

¹*The serpent was more crafty than any of the wild animals the Lord God had made. He said to the woman, "Did God really say, 'You must not eat from any tree in the garden'?"*

²*The woman said to the serpent, "We may eat fruit from the trees in the garden,* ³*but God did say, 'You must not eat fruit from the tree that is in the middle of the garden, and you must not touch it, or you will die.' "*

⁴*"You will not surely die," the serpent said to the woman.* ⁵*"For God knows that when you eat of it your eyes will be opened, and you will be like God, knowing good and evil."*

⁶*When the woman saw that the fruit of the tree was good for food and pleasing to the eye, and also desirable for gaining wisdom, she took some and ate it. She also gave some to her husband, who was with her, and he ate it.*

notes:

Summarize these introductory remarks. Be sure to include the underlined information, which gives the answers to the student book questions (provided in the margin).

What qualities should a football coach exhibit so that his players will "buy into" him as a leader?

According to the leader, why do so many people resist the commands and principles that God has given them?

Maximum _____ comes from _____ to God's rule in our lives.

...about today's session (5 minutes)

LETTING THE COACH BE IN CHARGE

The most successful football teams are those where the players "buy into" the coach's character, plans and personality. It is difficult for players to give their best effort when they don't trust the person in charge and his plans for the team. The same is true in our Christian lives. Until we "buy into" and really get to know the heart of God, we will resist the rules He sets down for us to follow.

God wants us to seek Him first and put His will foremost. As we seek him, placing ourselves under His authority is a delight! This was what the psalmist experienced in Psalm 119:10 and 12. "I seek you with all my heart; do not let me stray from your commands. ... Praise be to you, O Lord; teach me your decrees." Once we get a glimpse of the heart of God, His commands become a joy because we know and trust the One giving them.

Today's session will show us the value of placing our lives under God's authority. We will learn that maximum freedom comes from submitting to God's rule in our lives. Here's a picture of what happens when we try to exert our own authority instead of subjecting ourselves to the authority of someone who is more qualified:

"The lion was proud of his mastery of the animal kingdom. One day he decided to make sure all the other animals knew he was the king of the jungle. He was so confident that he bypassed the smaller animals and went straight to the bear. 'Who is the king of the jungle?' the lion asked. The bear replied, 'Why, you are, of course.' The lion gave a mighty roar of approval.

"Next he asked the tiger, 'Who is the king of the jungle?' The tiger quickly responded, 'Everyone knows that you are, O mighty lion.'

"Next on the list was the elephant. The lion faced the elephant and addressed his question: 'Who is the king of the jungle?' The elephant immediately grabbed the lion with his trunk, whirled him around in the air five or six times, and slammed him into a tree. Then he pounded him on the ground several times, dunked him under water in a nearby lake, and finally threw him onto the shore.

"The lion—beaten, bruised and battered—struggled to his feet. He looked at the elephant through sad and bloody eyes and said, 'Look, just because you don't know the answer is no reason for you to get mean about it!' "[1]

7

✝

Identifying with the Story (5-7 minutes)

⚘ Remain in groups of 6–8 people, in a horseshoe configuration.

In this small group session, students will be responding to the following questions that will help them share their stories in terms of the story of Adam and Eve's fall into sin in Genesis 2:15–17; 3:1–6.

Have the students explore these questions together.

1. Which of the following foods would tempt you the least if placed in a buffet line?

   ☐ broccoli   ☐ asparagus   ☐ artichoke
   ☐ cauliflower   ☐ cabbage   ☐ chicken liver
   ☐ other:_____

2. Which of God's commands did Satan have the most success getting you to question as a teenager?

   ☐ returning good for evil   ☐ honoring your parents
   ☐ not worrying about tomorrow   ☐ turning the other cheek
   ☐ storing up treasures in heaven   ☐ not judging others
   ☐ not worrying about your body or what you'll wear
   ☐ other:_____

3. Complete the following sentence: "I find that I'm most susceptible to temptation when ..."

   ☐ I neglect reading the Bible.   ☐ I'm tired.
   ☐ I neglect my prayer life.   ☐ I get busy.
   ☐ I'm alone.   ☐ I go shopping.
   ☐ Other:_____   ☐ I get bored.

notes:

today's session (15-20 minutes)

Share with your class the following information which you may modify according to your own perspectives and teaching needs. The answers to the student book questions (provided in the margin) are underlined.

According to the leader, how is living the Christian life different from moving into adulthood?

What sign of maturity did the leader mention regarding authority?

As children grow into their teenage years, they typically long for more freedom in their decision making. The last thing many of them want to hear is their parents' point-of-view. As they mature into adulthood, they naturally step out from the umbrella of authority their parents had been exercising over them for their entire lives. The Christian life, however, is somewhat different where authority is concerned. Many Christians think they can make wise decisions without placing themselves under God's authority. In other words, God doesn't have the "last say" in a matter. However, maturity in our Christian lives is not marked by our ability to make our own choices. Rather, a sign of maturity is seen in our willingness to place our lives under the umbrella of God's authority, as we make choices that coincide with God's will and direction for our lives.

The problem that many of us encounter is that we don't like to be told what to do. As children, we didn't like to be told to share our toys or do our chores. This resistance to authority remains a struggle for many into adulthood. For example, many people stop going to church because they don't want to be told "no." They think Christianity is about putting rules in their lives and prohibiting any fun. Most likely, they feel their lives are already filled with too many rules. The last thing they want is to subject themselves to more rules.

What happens when we try to seek freedom by resisting God's authority?

How does Proverbs 14:12 speak to the issue of being our own authority?

As a result, many choose a path they think will lead to more freedom in their lives. In doing so, they actually lose freedom. Proverbs 14:12 speaks to this issue when it says, "There is a way that seems right to a man, but in the end it leads to death." Our society wants us to believe that freedom is gained by moving out from under anyone's authority. The exact opposite is true, though. In the same way that a train has the most power and freedom when it stays on the tracks, we experience the most power and freedom when we submit ourselves to God's authority. In today's session, we will learn that maximum freedom is gained only when we place ourselves under God's authority.

What was the one rule that God instituted in the garden of Eden?

In Genesis 2:15–17, we see the way God wanted the world to be. In God's original design, man and woman would exist without interference from sin. Adam and Eve were living in a world very similar to the kind of world most of us want, which is a world without rules. In verses 16–17, God says, "You are free to eat from any tree in the garden; but you must not eat from the tree of the knowledge of good and evil, for when you eat of it you will surely die." God gave them only one rule. We see from God's original plan that He is into freedom. In the beginning, Adam and Eve lived in a one-rule world. Adam had great freedom; he could even name the animals whatever he wanted. God was the one who established Adam's freedom

7

today's session (cont'd)

and right to rule. As long as Adam functioned under God's authority, he would live in a one-rule world. Contrary to what some may think, God did not take man's freedom away. When people talk about God or religion, you often hear that God is the one who has taken away their freedom. What we learn from this story is that sin took away our freedom. The truth is that maximum freedom is found under God's authority, not outside it.

In Genesis 3:1–6, we read the account of the serpent tempting the woman to eat of the forbidden fruit. In verse 1, the serpent says, "Did God really say, 'You must not eat from any tree in the garden'?" Immediately, Satan questions what God has said. The woman knew what God had said and tells the serpent, "We may eat fruit from the trees in the garden, but God did say, 'You must not eat fruit from the tree that is in the middle of the garden, and you must not touch it, or you will die.' " So, the serpent tries another angle and seeks to get the woman to think that God can't be trusted. In verse 4, the serpent tells her, "You will not surely die … . For God knows that when you eat of it your eyes will be opened, and you will be like God, knowing good and evil." The serpent wanted the woman to believe that God was hiding something good from her and didn't want her to have it. The serpent even provided the way to get it—disobedience. The serpent's ploy was that she could be absolutely free if she lived in a "no-rule" world. All she would have to do is step out from God's authority. The woman took the bait and disobeyed along with the man. The question we need to ask is, "Did they gain freedom or lose freedom?" The answer is obvious—they lost it. Adam and Eve moved from a "one-rule" world to a multi-rule world. They lost the freedom to live in the garden, to live in a world with no pain, to live in a world without disease, to be free of guilt, to relate to God without sin, to experience relationships without conflict, and to live without sin. They gained a world that had many rules. Why did God add more rules? Because any time we are in a dangerous place, rules are established for our protection. It wasn't God who caused this multi-rule world. It was humanity's freedom and humanity's choice to sin.

Did Adam and Eve gain freedom or lose freedom by disobeying God and being their own authority?

The question we have to answer is, "Can God be trusted?" not, "Will I live under rules?" Sin results in the loss of freedom in all areas of our lives. Some people lose freedom in marriage due to adultery, in their finances due to poor spending habits, and in what they say and watch because of their earthly nature, a nature that is not influenced by God. We don't gain freedom by ignoring God's rules and authority. In fact, we lose it. Our greatest regrets in life most likely could have been avoided if we had been living under God's authority. People think God enjoys rules. On the contrary, God gave us laws not to restrict our freedom, but to protect it. The most liberated marriages are those that live under God's law and authority. The rules He has established are there to preserve our freedom.

According to the leader, why do so many Christians still hesitate to submit to God's authority in their lives?

Why do we still hesitate to live under God's authority? Why do we hesitate in submitting ourselves to God? <u>The reason is that rules apart from a relationship always lead to a lack of trust and, consequently, rebellion</u>. If a lawgiver we don't have a relationship with requires us to do something we don't agree with, we will be hesitant to trust the lawgiver. One of the reasons many people have a hard time submitting to God is because their relationship with God has become almost void. The result is that they have a hard time trusting God. They stop investing in the relationship. When the relationship dissipates, the obedience dissipates. When we trust someone absolutely and they set up a rule, we're more likely to submit to it. As we grow in trust, we'll grow in obedience. We need to embrace a relationship with the "rule giver," rather than the rules themselves. How we perceive God's rules has everything to do with how we perceive God. Seeing God's rules for what they are only comes when we see God for who He is. We need to see that God has put up fences to protect us, rather than to restrict our freedom. When we develop a relationship with God first, and then place our lives under His authority, we'll experience the freedom we have always desired.

notes:

7

✝

♞ Remain in groups of 6–8 people, in a horseshoe configuration.

In this small-group session, students will be applying the lessons of the text to their own lives through the following questions.

The students were asked (in the student book) to choose an answer for each question and explain why.

Learning from the Story (5-7 minutes)

1. Why do you think God made sure Adam and Eve understood the consequences of disobeying Him and eating from the tree of the knowledge of good and evil?

   ☐ God wanted to protect them.
   ☐ God wanted to show them His justice.
   ☐ God wanted to prepare them for temptation.
   ☐ God wanted them to look beyond momentary pleasures.
   ☐ God wanted them to understand the severity of sin.
   ☐ God wanted them to appreciate the freedom that He had given them.
   ☐ Other:_____

2. When Satan begins whispering in your ear to disobey God, what should you do first?

   ☐ Ask your friends what you should do.
   ☐ Ask yourself what Oprah or Ann Landers would do.
   ☐ Ask yourself what Jesus would do.
   ☐ Ask God for wisdom.
   ☐ Ask God for strength.
   ☐ Think about the potential consequences.
   ☐ Think of a Bible verse that speaks to the temptation.
   ☐ Try to stop thinking about it.
   ☐ Other:_____

3. What lie or false promise does Satan use most when tempting you?

notes:

life change lessons (5-7 minutes)

Share with the class the following thoughts on how the lessons of this text might be applied today. The answers to the student book questions (provided in the margin) are underlined unless the question requires a personal answer.

What are some of the pros and cons associated with living under someone else's authority?

Which one of God's commands or principles do you have the most trouble following in your life? Why?

What is your plan for investing in your relationship with God this week?

Most of our lives we have no choice about living under someone else's authority. We were born into a family with parents who raised us under their authority. We go to school where teachers hold authority over their students. We get jobs where the employer holds authority over their employees. We live in a society where government holds authority over us and establishes laws that all citizens have to follow. Living under God's authority, however, is a choice that each of us must make. What are some practical things you can do to begin living under God's authority? Here are three steps you can take:

1. MAKE A LIST OF THE PROS AND CONS OF BEING UNDER SOMEONE ELSE'S AUTHORITY. Think about all of the authority figures in your life. List them in one column on a sheet of paper. Then, beside the first column, begin listing the obvious pros and cons that you associate with each authority figure. Examples of authority figures include policemen, employer, pastor, parent, etc.

2. MAKE A LIST OF GOD'S COMMANDS IN SCRIPTURE THAT YOU FIND THE MOST DIFFICULT TO FOLLOW AND ASK GOD TO GIVE YOU A WILLINGNESS TO OBEY THEM. There may be some of Jesus' commands that you find difficult to follow or are unwilling to follow. List those commands and ask yourself what He's trying to protect you from or what He's trying to provide for you. You may be amazed at the answers you come up with.

3. INVEST IN A DAILY TIME WITH GOD, GETTING TO KNOW HIM BETTER. None of us like to be under the authority of someone we don't know and trust. The same is true with God. When you get to know God's heart, you can grow in your willingness to follow the commands and principles He's outlined in Scripture. Spend time each day this week with God gaining vital insights from the Bible and prayer, getting to know Him on a more intimate basis.

7

notes:

⟳ **CARING TIME**
Remain in groups of 6–8 people, in a horseshoe configuration.

Hand out the Prayer/ Praise Report to the entire group. Ask each subgroup to pray for the empty chair. Pray specifically for God to guide you to someone to bring next week to fill that chair.

After a sufficient time of prayer in subgroups, close in a corporate prayer. Say, "Next week we will talk about: 'Choosing to Study God's Word.' "

Remind participants of the daily Scripture readings and reflective questions found on page 92

Caring Time   (15-20 minutes)

During this time of caring for one another, pray that God will give each group member discernment concerning his or her responses to question 3 under "Learning from the Story." In addition, pray for the concerns on the Prayer/Praise Report.

Have each subgroup conclude their prayer time by reading 1 Corinthians 10:13 together:

No temptation has seized you except what is common to man. And God is faithful; he will not let you be tempted beyond what you can bear. But when you are tempted, he will also provide a way out so that you can stand up under it.

notes:

BIBLE STUDY NOTES

Reference Notes

Use these notes to gain further understanding
of the text as you study on your own.

GENESIS 2:15

work ... take care. Work was part of God's plan from the beginning. Man was given the responsibility of being an obedient servant and wise steward.

GENESIS 2:16

any tree. God gave Adam the freedom to choose which tree he would eat from. This included the tree of life mentioned in Genesis 2:9.

GENESIS 2:17
knowledge

tree of the knowledge of good and evil. This tree was placed in the garden to give Adam and Eve the opportunity to exercise their freedom of choice. Every tree was appealing, but only one was off limits. This "tree" gave them the opportunity to express their obedience and trust in God. The presence of evil was not in the substance of the fruit itself. They sinned in their attempt to gain God's knowledge independently of Him.

**GENESIS 2:17
(cont'd)**

surely die. Disobeying God results in spiritual death and ultimately physical death. The eating of the forbidden fruit in itself would not result in death. The act of disobedience to God that prompted taking the fruit brought death.

GENESIS 3:1

the serpent. While Satan is not referred to in this story, Revelation 12:9 and 20:2 identify Satan with the serpent.

**GENESIS 3:3
choice**

the tree that is in the middle of the garden. This was the tree of the knowledge of good and evil (Gen. 2:9,17). Popular depictions show it as an apple tree, but Scripture does not identify it with any known fruit. Why was the tree there if God did not want them to eat of it? Perhaps because God wanted people to have a choice about whether to obey Him or not.
or you will die. The clear implication is that God did not originally intend people to have to experience even physical death. Physical death came as a result of human sin (see Rom. 5:12–14).

**GENESIS 3:5
remain in truth**

you will be like God. This is the basis of much of the temptation we face—that we try to be like God. Specific situations in the Bible where this was the case include the Tower of Babel (Gen. 11:1–9), God's answer to Job (Job 40:6–41:34), and Christ's third temptation (Matt. 4:8–9). And a prime example is Lucifer's (Satan's) rebellion in heaven that caused him to be cast out of God's presence (Isa. 14:12–15).

notes:

7

[1] James S. Hewitt, editor, *Illustrations Unlimited* (Wheaton, IL: Tyndale House Publishers, 1988), 312.

Session

8

Choosing to
Study God's Word

Prepare for the Session

	READINGS	REFLECTIVE QUESTIONS
Monday	Psalm 19:7–8	How does the Bible revive your soul?
Tuesday	Psalm 19:9–10	How is the Word of God described in these verses? Could you say this about God's Word in your own life?
Wednesday	Psalm 19:11	What warning in God's Word has protected you from making the wrong decisions?
Thursday	James 1:22	How have you applied the Word of God to your life this week?
Friday	James 1:23	How does the Bible act as a mirror, revealing your true self?
Saturday	James 1:24	What have you learned about yourself from the Bible this week? How can you make sure you don't forget what you've learned?
Sunday	James 1:25	What are the conditions this verse places on being blessed? How well are you meeting those conditions?

notes:

OUR GOALS FOR
THIS SESSION ARE:

**∪ In groups of 6–8,
gather people in
a horseshoe
configuration.**

**Make sure everyone
has a name tag.**

**Take time to share
information on class
parties that are coming
up as well as any
relevant church events.**

**INTRODUCE THE
ICEBREAKER ACTIVITY:
The students have
been given instructions
in their books.**

**After the Icebreaker
say something like,
"As we drive our cars
and go about our
days, there are many
sights and sounds
that vie for our atten-
tion. In today's ses-
sion, we'll discuss
the importance of
giving God's Word
plenty of time and
attention, enabling
us to overcome a
lot of the 'road noise'
of life."**

**Hand out the
Prayer/Praise Report.
A sample copy is
on pages 158-159.
Have people write
down prayer requests
and praises. Then
have the prayer
coordinator collect
the report and make
copies for use during
the Caring Time.**

BIBLE STUDY	• to understand the benefits of reading and studying the Bible
	• to know how to effectively read and study the Bible
	• to learn the importance of applying the truths of the Bible to our lives
LIFE CHANGE	• to take notes when hearing God's Word taught or preached in our church
	• to make a plan for regularly reading and studying the Bible
	• to keep a journal for recording what we learn from studying the Bible

Icebreaker   (10-15 minutes)

Road Noise. Many people spend a large amount of time in their cars commuting to work or running errands. Which of the following do you find yourself listening to the most when driving?

☐ news radio

☐ political talk radio

☐ sports talk radio

☐ pop/rock music

☐ classical music

☐ my own tape/CD collection

☐ contemporary Christian music

☐ gospel music

☐ oldies music

☐ country music

☐ R & B music

☐ cell phone

☐ other:_____

8

notes:

Bible Study   (30-45 minutes)

The Scripture for this week:

[22]Do not merely listen to the word, and so deceive yourselves. Do what it says. [23]Anyone who listens to the word but does not do what it says is like a man who looks at his face in a mirror [24]and, after looking at himself, goes away and immediately forgets what he looks like. [25]But the man who looks intently into the perfect law that gives freedom, and continues to do this, not forgetting what he has heard, but doing it—he will be blessed in what he does.

LEARNING FROM THE BIBLE

JAMES 1:22–25

Have a member of the class, selected ahead of time, read the passage from James.

notes:

Summarize these introductory remarks. Be sure to include the underlined information, which gives the answers to the student book questions (provided in the margin).

Why do most football teams develop playbooks?

According to the leader, what do too many Christians underestimate the importance of?

...about today's session (5 minutes)

READING GOD'S PLAYBOOK

Most football teams develop a playbook that contains the offensive and defensive plays they plan to use against their opponents. <u>These are the plays that they feel will give them the greatest chance of success</u>. As coaches develop plays for their team, they take into consideration their team's strengths and weaknesses in light of who their opponent will be. In life, God has given each of us a "playbook" that is designed to help us succeed against our opponent in all the situations we will face in life. One of the first things that new players must do when joining a new team is learn the team's playbook. As Christians, we should have a similar priority. While some people gain much knowledge about our "playbook," the Bible, <u>too many underestimate the importance of applying God's Word to their own lives</u>. Here's a story that illustrates this point:

"A church member consistently met him (the pastor) after the service and said, 'You sure preached to them today.' The pastor frequently dreamed of some day hearing this woman take the message personally. He thought he had finally gotten his chance when a severe storm prevented all but the pastor and this woman from showing up one Sunday. After the message he knew she couldn't quote her standard remark. Indeed she didn't. She said, 'Too bad they weren't all here because … . You sure preached to them today.' "[1]

Today's session will help us understand the importance of applying God's Word to our lives.

notes:

✝

Identifying with the Story (5-7 minutes)

⊍ Remain in groups of 6–8 people, in a horseshoe configuration.

In this small group session, students will be responding to the following questions that will help them share their stories in the words of James regarding the application of God's truth in their lives.

Have the students explore these questions together.

1. Which of the following phrases best describes how you listened in class during your high school days?

   passing notes · · · · · · · · · · · · · · · · · taking notes

   nodding off · · · · · · · · · · · · · · · · · speaking up

   back row · · · · · · · · · · · · · · · · · · · front row

2. Would you describe yourself as a better listener or a better talker? Explain.

3. Finish the sentence: "A time when I should have listened and responded to what God was trying to tell me to do but didn't was …"

8

Share with your class the following information which you may modify according to your own perspectives and teaching needs. The answers to the student book questions (provided in the margin) are underlined.

What was the general purpose of the book of James?

What three advantages did the leader give from James 1:22–25 for reading and studying the Bible?

According to the leader, what can we do to avoid living a wasted life?

How does the Bible produce freedom in our lives?

According to James, what should we do to be "blessed" in what we do?

today's session (15-20 minutes)

The reason for James' letter was to respond to those who claimed Christ as Lord but were not showing it in their lives. The focus is on doing what the Bible teaches us to do, not just knowing what the Bible guides us to do. In James 1:22–25, we gain great insight into why and how to connect God's Word to our lives. Here are some advantages of reading and studying the Bible, God's "playbook" for life.

One advantage to reading and studying God's Word is that we avoid a wasted life when we believe it and obey it. In verse 22, James writes, "Do not merely listen to the word, and so deceive yourselves." James warns us about being a casual listener to God's Word. If we think that attending church services and programs are all we need to grow spiritually mature, we're only fooling ourselves. Many Christians end up wasting their lives because they were never serious about living out their faith. So, how do we avoid living a wasted life? We must believe God's Word to such an extent that we live it by faith each day. If all we do is listen but fail to abide by the truth of God's Word, we are deceiving ourselves and wasting our time. God's Word holds the answers for how we can make the most of our lives for God. We are wise when we believe it and do it.

A second advantage to reading God's Word is that we gain freedom when we follow it. In verse 25, James describes Scripture as "the perfect law that gives freedom." James tells us that the "perfect law," which is the spiritual, moral, and ethical teachings found in the Bible and fulfilled in Jesus Christ, do not restrict us but, rather, give us greater freedom and joy. This supports what Jesus taught in John 8:31–32, " 'If you hold to my teaching, you are really my disciples. Then you will know the truth, and the truth will set you free' ." In the same way a locomotive has its greatest freedom and power when it stays on its tracks, we experience freedom when we follow the teachings of God's Word. When we live life the way we think it should be lived, apart from the truth of God's Word, the result is a lack of freedom and often a train wreck.

A third advantage to reading God's Word is that we bear spiritual fruit when we stay with it. In verse 25, James says that the person who continues to study ("looks intently") God's Word "will be blessed in what he does." We bear spiritual fruit such as faith and love when we keep our hearts open and receptive to our source of life, Christ. In John 15:5, Jesus declared, "I am the vine; you are the branches. If a man remains in me and I in him, he will bear much fruit; apart from me you can do nothing." When we stay connected in fellowship with Christ and follow His truth, our lives will bear abundant spiritual fruit. We can't expect to produce fruit with no

96

root! Our lives must stay grounded in God's Word and in our walk with Christ daily if we are going to accomplish all God has for us.

James also shows us how to effectively read our "playbook" for life. First, he says we should study it carefully. In verse 25, James describes the person who will benefit from God's Word as "the man who looks intently into the perfect law." How can we move from merely listening to God's Word to studying God's Word? Studying God's Word means we take our time in understanding the original meaning of the text. This will involve asking the right kind of questions that will shed light on its meaning. We should be aware of the author's identity, the time era when he was writing, the customs and culture in which he was writing, and who the intended readers were. Discovering these answers means that we must have access to a good study Bible and a Bible commentary or Bible dictionary among other resources. As we gain insight to the Scriptures we're reading, a good habit is to write down what we're learning in the margin of our Bibles or in journals.

The second instruction James gives is for us to memorize it strategically. In describing the person who benefits from God's Word, James says they work on "not forgetting what [they have] heard" (v. 25). It's easy to memorize the things that we want to remember. For instance, all of us know our street address, a friend's phone number, sports statistics, words to songs we like, etc. Knowing the truths of God's Word in our minds and hearts helps us fight against the sins to which we are most susceptible (Heb. 12:1). In Psalm 119:11, the psalmist writes, "I have hidden your word in my heart that I might not sin against you." In order to be prepared for troubling temptations, we can memorize verses that will encourage us to obey Christ, rather than the false promises of sin. Remembering what God has said also helps us make wise decisions in life.

What are three advantages to memorizing Scripture?

8

Again, the psalmist writes, "Your word is a lamp to my feet and a light for my path" (Ps. 119:105). God's Word sheds light on decisions we're facing and shows us the right path through life. Memorizing Scripture also aids our ability to share our faith in Christ with others. Peter tells us to "Always be prepared to give an answer to everyone who asks you to give the reason for the hope that you have" (1 Peter 3:15). Knowing the Scriptures that explain the basic truths of forgiveness, a new life, and an eternal existence in heaven enhances our ability to share the truth about Christ's offer of salvation.

The third and most effective way to make sure we benefit from God's "playbook" is to apply it daily. In verse 22, James instructs us to, "Do what it says." And in verse 25, he reinforces the importance of application for the person who wants to benefit from God's Word. As this person continues "doing it [obeying God's Word]—he will be blessed in what he does."

today's session (cont'd)

Applying God's Word is a three-step process. <u>We first need to under-stand what the Scripture meant to the original hearers.</u> The only way to do this effectively is to study the background of the passage. <u>The second step involves pulling out the timeless principle held in the passage that holds true for all people, in all places, at all times. The third step is asking God to show us how to apply that principle in our own lives.</u> As we apply God's Word to our lives and follow Christ and His truth, we will find wisdom for making the critical decisions we're faced with every day.

What are the three steps involved in applying God's Word to our lives?

✠

Learning from the Story (5-7 minutes)

✺ *Remain in groups of 6–8 people, in a horseshoe configuration.*

In this small-group session, students will be applying the lessons of the text to their own lives through the following questions.

The students were asked (in the student book) to choose an answer for each question and explain why.

1. After hearing a sermon in my church, most people generally think the following:

   ☐ "That was a nice sermon. Now, back to life as usual."
   ☐ "I sure hope so and so was listening. They really needed to hear that!"
   ☐ "I really needed to hear that message and I probably need to act on it ... one day."
   ☐ "I've carried out my weekly duty to appease God. Now, to more important things."
   ☐ "God was really speaking to me today."
   ☐ Other:_____

2. Based on James 1:22–25, what word do you think best describes the people James was writing this letter to?

   ☐ lazy   ☐ prideful   ☐ worldly
   ☐ busy   ☐ religious   ☐ hypocritical
   ☐ other:_____

3. Which of the following areas of hearing God's Word that James mentions do you struggle with the most?

   ☐ depth of studying the Bible—"looks intently into the perfect law"
   ☐ consistency in reading and studying the Bible—"continues to do this"
   ☐ memorizing Scripture—"not forgetting what he has heard"
   ☐ applying Scripture to my life—"doing it"

notes:

Share with the class the following thoughts on how the lessons of this text might be applied today. The answers to the student book questions (provided in the margin) are underlined unless the question requires a personal answer.

What are two primary differences between being a hearer and a doer of God's Word?

What are three things you can do to start applying God's Word to your life?

life change lessons (5-7 minutes)

Reading the Bible and listening to Bible teaching are much easier than actually acting on the truths presented in the Bible. The difference between being a hearer and a doer is <u>expectation and intent</u>. First, do you expect God to speak to you personally through the Bible? Second, do you have a teachable spirit that is eager to obey whatever God tells you through His Word? Let's be "doers of the word" as James suggests. Here are some things you can do to start applying God's Word to your life:

1. <u>TAKE NOTES WHEN HEARING GOD'S WORD TAUGHT AND PREACHED IN YOUR CHURCH</u>. Studies have shown that we typically forget about 95 percent of what we hear after 72 hours. One way to combat our forgetfulness is to write down the truths and insights we glean from the teaching and preaching of the Bible in our church. Make it a habit to bring a pen and a journal or paper with you every time the Bible is taught in your church. As you take notes, write down what God is teaching you and how you might apply it to your own life.

2. <u>MAKE A PLAN FOR REGULARLY READING AND STUDYING THE BIBLE</u>. Local Christian bookstores contain many devotional books and Bibles with reading plans that help you consistently read and study Scripture. You might start by reading one chapter per day, with the goal of reading through the entire New Testament. Plans for reading the entire Bible in one year are readily available.

3. <u>KEEP A JOURNAL FOR RECORDING WHAT YOU LEARN FROM STUDYING THE BIBLE</u>. As you spend your personal time in the Bible, make it a habit to write down the things you are learning and how God wants you to apply these things in your life. Some people write down thoughts in the margin of their Bible. Others use a blank journal. Keeping a journal can encourage you later on in life as you look back at how you've grown in your faith and see how God has worked in your life.

8

Caring Time (15-20 minutes)

CARING TIME
Remain in groups
of 6–8 people, in
a horseshoe
configuration.

Hand out the Prayer/
Praise Report to the
entire group. Ask each
subgroup to pray for
the empty chair. Pray
specifically for God to
guide you to someone
to bring next week to
fill that chair.

After a sufficient
time of prayer in
subgroups, close in
a corporate prayer.
Say, "Next week we
will talk about:
'Choosing the Holy
Spirit's Guidance.'"

Remind participants
of the daily Scripture
readings and reflective
questions found on
page 102.

During this time of caring, pray that each member of the group will become more disciplined in studying God's Word—not only in receiving God's Word through hearing, reading, and memorizing, but also in the practical application of it in life. In addition, pray for the concerns on the Prayer/Praise Report.

Have each group close by reading Psalm 19:7–11 together:
> The law of the Lord is perfect,
>   reviving the soul.
> The statutes of the Lord are trustworthy,
>   making wise the simple.
> The precepts of the Lord are right,
>   giving joy to the heart.
> The commands of the Lord are radiant,
>   giving light to the eyes.
> The fear of the Lord is pure,
>   enduring forever.
> The ordinances of the Lord are sure
>   and altogether righteous.
> They are more precious than gold,
>   than much pure gold;
> they are sweeter than honey,
>   than honey from the comb.
> By them is your servant warned;
>   in keeping them there is great reward.

notes:

BIBLE STUDY NOTES

Reference Notes

Use these notes to gain further understanding
of the text as you study on your own.

JAMES 1:22
response

merely listen. The Christian must not just hear the Word of God. A response is required.

deceive yourselves. To make mere knowledge of God's will the sole criterion for the religious life is dangerous and self-deceptive.

Do what it says. This is James' main point in this section.

JAMES 1:23–24
change

James illustrates his point with a metaphor. The person who reads Scripture (which is a mirror to the Christian, because in it his or her true state is shown), and then goes away unchanged is like the person who gets up in the morning and sees how dirty and disheveled he or she is, but then promptly forgets about it (when the proper response would be to get cleaned up).

JAMES 1:25
blessing

the perfect law. The reference is probably to the teachings of Jesus that set one free, in contrast to the Jewish law, which brought bondage (see Rom. 8:2).

continues. Such people make obedience to the gospel a continuing part of their lives.

blessed. The sheer act of keeping this law is a happy experience in and of itself because it produces good fruit, now and in the future.

notes:

8

[1] Raymond McHenry, ed., *The Best of in Other Words* (Houston, TX: Raymond McHenry, 1996), 31.

Session 9

Choosing the Holy Spirit's Guidance

Prepare for the Session

	READINGS	REFLECTIVE QUESTIONS
Monday	John 16:5–6	Do you ever lack an awareness of God in your life?
Tuesday	John 16:7–8	Who do you usually go to for wise counsel? Do you ever ask the Holy Spirit for counsel?
Wednesday	John 16:9	How does sin prevent people from knowing Christ?
Thursday	John 16:10	When have you struggled with knowing right from wrong?
Friday	John 16:11	What does it mean to you that the "prince of the world," Satan, already stands condemned?
Saturday	John 16:12–13	What truth from the Bible do you struggle to believe?
Sunday	John 16:14–16	How does the Spirit make known to you Christ's desires in your life?

notes:

OUR GOALS FOR THIS SESSION ARE:

⊍ In groups of 6–8, gather people in a horseshoe configuration.

Make sure everyone has a name tag.

Take time to share information on class parties that are coming up as well as any relevant church events.

INTRODUCE THE ICEBREAKER ACTIVITY: The students have been given instructions in their books.

After the Icebreaker say something like, "Following directions, instead of trying to figure everything out on our own, can make life much smoother and easier. Today, we will talk about the importance and benefits of following the Holy Spirit's direction in our lives."

Hand out the Prayer/Praise Report. A sample copy is on pages 158–159. Have people write down prayer requests and praises. Then have the prayer coordinator collect the report and make copies for use during the Caring Time.

BIBLE STUDY
· to learn the role of the Holy Spirit in the world
· to see the reasons we should follow the Holy Spirit's guidance in our lives
· to understand how the Holy Spirit guides us through internal "promptings"

LIFE CHANGE
· to put up our "spiritual antennas" each day and listen for the Spirit's "promptings"
· to keep a journal of the Spirit's "promptings" in our lives each day this week
· to pray that God will give us His peace in the critical decisions we are facing

Icebreaker (10-15 minutes)

Following Directions. Which one of the following sources of directions are you most likely to follow (mark it with an **X**) and which one are you least likely to follow (mark it with a ✔)? Explain your answers.

- ☐ my spouse
- ☐ a recipe book
- ☐ my boss
- ☐ the owner's manual to my car
- ☐ speed limit signs
- ☐ signs leading to a yard sale
- ☐ the directions for assembling a dollhouse
- ☐ a convenience store worker when I am driving and can't find my way
- ☐ other:_____

9

notes:

✝

**Have a member of
the class, selected
ahead of time, read
the passage from
John.**

Bible Study   (30-45 minutes)

The Scripture for this week:

[5]"Now I am going to him who sent me, yet none of you asks me, 'Where are you going?' [6]Because I have said these things, you are filled with grief. [7]But I tell you the truth: It is for your good that I am going away. Unless I go away, the Counselor will not come to you; but if I go, I will send him to you. [8]When he comes, he will convict the world of guilt in regard to sin and righteousness and judgment: [9]in regard to sin, because men do not believe in me; [10]in regard to righteousness, because I am going to the Father, where you can see me no longer; [11]and in regard to judgment, because the prince of this world now stands condemned.

[12]"I have much more to say to you, more than you can now bear. [13]But when he, the Spirit of truth, comes, he will guide you into all truth. He will not speak on his own; he will speak only what he hears, and he will tell you what is yet to come. [14]He will bring glory to me by taking from what is mine and making it known to you. [15]All that belongs to the Father is mine. That is why I said the Spirit will take from what is mine and make it known to you.

[16]"In a little while you will see me no more, and then after a little while you will see me."

**Summarize these
introductory remarks.
Be sure to include
the underlined
information, which
gives the answers
to the student book
questions (provided
in the margin).**

*According to the
leader, what is the
key to following
Jesus each day?*

...about today's session (5 minutes)

FOLLOWING THE PLAY CALLING

On professional football teams, every quarterback is equipped with a speaker in his helmet. When the coach calls in the next play for the offense, he uses a radio to communicate it to the quarterback. Once the quarterback hears what play is called, he huddles the offensive players together, relays the play to them and then carries out the instructions of his coach. This is similar to our role as followers of Christ. God has called us to follow His voice and carry out His instructions for our lives. In John 10:27, Jesus said, " 'My sheep listen to my voice; I know them, and they follow me.' " <u>The key to following Jesus is hearing His voice as we walk in a close relationship with Him.</u> God has not placed a speaker in our helmet, but He has placed His Spirit in our lives.

In today's session, we will focus on how the Holy Spirit guides us in our everyday lives. We have a choice. We can choose to ignore the promptings of the Spirit in our lives or we can listen to God's voice and follow the Spirit. In Hebrews 3: 7–8,15, the following words are found twice for good reason: "Today, if you hear his voice do not harden your hearts." Each time we fail to recognize or refuse to follow the Spirit's voice in our lives, our hearts will grow harder. Many Christians prefer to call their own "plays" and live their lives according to their own desires. Making the right choices when faced with critical decisions becomes easier when we remember the following truth: Our role is not to call our own "plays," but to follow the instructions given to us by the Holy Spirit.

What is the result of ignoring the Spirit's voice in our lives?

notes:

⊕

Identifying with the Story (5-7 minutes)

⊙ Remain in groups of 6–8 people, in a horseshoe configuration.

In this small group session, students' responses to the following questions will help them share their stories in terms of Jesus' words about the Holy Spirit in John 16:5–16.

Have the students explore these questions together.

1. When has someone you loved gone away for an extended period of time? How did you stay encouraged during his or her absence?

2. If you had been one of the disciples, what would have been the most difficult thing about Jesus leaving you after three years?

   ☐ the inability to talk directly with Jesus
   ☐ having to follow someone I couldn't see anymore
   ☐ having to endure suffering similar to what Jesus experienced
   ☐ no longer sharing our meals and lives together
   ☐ missing the encouragement of Jesus who believed in me so much
   ☐ wondering what to do next now that He was gone
   ☐ other:_____

3. Which of the following "departures" was the most difficult for you growing up?

   ☐ graduating from high school and leaving my friends
   ☐ leaving home and living on my own for the first time
   ☐ leaving home for college
   ☐ having my best friend move away
   ☐ moving to a new town or city while still in high school
   ☐ breaking up with a boyfriend or girlfriend
   ☐ other:_____

9

Share with your class the following information which you may modify according to your own perspectives and teaching needs. The answers to the student book questions (provided in the margin) are underlined.

today's session (15-20 minutes)

Have you ever had the experience of getting a new car, getting out on the road, and then noticing that you're not the only one driving a car just like yours? When you come out of a shopping mall, you are quick to spot cars of similar make. As you drive down the road, you begin to think everybody has a car just like yours! In the same way, when we accept Christ and His Spirit comes to reside in our hearts, we begin to notice Him working around us in ways we haven't noticed before. We begin to sense His voice prompting us. This should be the norm for believers. In Galatians 5:25, the apostle Paul writes, "Since we live by the Spirit, let us keep in step with the Spirit." In order to be led by the Spirit, we must first recognize Him and His work in our lives.

As Jesus prepared to go to the cross, He wanted His disciples to know they would not be left alone in the world. In our Scripture passage today, John 16:5–16, we find Jesus leaving some encouraging words to His disciples prior to His death. In verse 6, we see that Jesus was aware of His disciples' need for encouragement: " 'Because I have said these things, you are filled with grief.' " Surely, the disciples would wonder how they would carry on without Jesus in the up-and-down world they were living in. In verse 7, Jesus comforted them with the promise of the Counselor who would come and help them: " 'I tell you the truth: It is for your good that I am going away.' " We know from John 14:26 that Jesus is referring to the Holy Spirit. Even before His ascension, Jesus reassured us of His continuing presence through the Holy Spirit with these words: "And surely I am with you always, to the very end of the age" (Matt. 28:20).

What three roles did Jesus say the Holy Spirit would play in the world?

In John 16:8–11, Jesus describes the role that the Holy Spirit will play in the world. First, the Holy Spirit helps us recognize our need for God. In verses 8–9, Jesus said, " 'When he comes, he will convict the world of guilt in regard to sin … because men do not believe in me.' " The first role of the Holy Spirit is to convince those who are not yet believers of their need for a relationship with God. Earlier, in John 6:44, Jesus said, "No one can come to me unless the Father who sent me draws him."

Not only does the Spirit make us aware that we are separated from God because of our sin, but that Christ is the answer for our separation from God. In verse 10, Jesus says the Spirit will convict the world, " 'in regard to righteousness, because I am going to the Father, where you can see me no longer.' " The Spirit works in the conscience of individuals revealing truth. Many, however, suppress the truth and follow their own way. In Romans 1:18–19, we see there are "men who suppress the truth by their wickedness, since what may be known about God is plain to them, because God has made it plain to them."

The third aspect of the Spirit's work in the world is that He reminds us of God's attitude toward sin. In verse 11, Jesus says the Spirit will convict the world, "in regard to judgment, because the prince of this world now stands condemned." The Holy Spirit shows us the consequences of disobeying God's Word. God will judge all evil, including Satan himself.

Beginning in verse 13, Jesus specifically addresses the role the Spirit would play in the lives of the disciples. Speaking to His disciples in John 14:26, Jesus said that in His absence, the Spirit " 'will teach you all things and will remind you of everything I have said to you.' " In the same way Jesus taught and guided the disciples, the Spirit would also teach and guide them.

According to John 14:26, what would the Holy Spirit do for the disciples when Jesus was gone?

According to Jesus, we should heed the Holy Spirit for several reasons. First, the Holy Spirit guides us rather than forcing Himself upon us. In verse 13, referring to the Holy Spirit, Jesus said, "He will guide you." He will, however, control our thoughts and actions only to the point that we relinquish control. As we look for guidance in the decisions we make in life each day, the Spirit is there to help us make the right ones. We should also follow the Spirit's guidance because He can be trusted. In verse 13, Jesus says that when the Spirit guides us, we can trust Him because He will guide us "into all truth." "The function of the Spirit," writes Bernard Ramm, "is not to communicate new truth or to instruct in matters unknown, but to illuminate what is revealed in Scripture."[1] A third reason that God's children should follow the Spirit's guidance is because the Spirit speaks the words of our caring heavenly Father. In verse 13, Jesus said the Holy Spirit will "not speak on his own; he will speak only what he hears" from the Father. The Spirit's guidance will always be in line with that of a loving heavenly Father who seeks to protect His children from harm and give them what is good (see Matt. 7:11).

What are three reasons for following the Holy Spirit's guidance?

The Holy Spirit uses such instruments as Scripture, godly counsel, and prayer to communicate with believers. In this Bible study series we are taking a close look at each of these areas. The Spirit also guides us through His internal promptings in our lives. As we are faced with critical decisions, we can sense His guidance in two ways.

What are some of the most common tools the Holy Spirit uses to communicate with believers?

The first way we can sense His guidance is through the peace He gives to our hearts. In Colossians 3:15, the apostle Paul encouraged us to, "Let the peace of Christ rule in your hearts." In other words, the peace that the Spirit brings should serve as an umpire in our hearts, letting us know when we're in or out of bounds according to God's will and Word. When we accept Christ as Savior and Lord, we

In what two ways does the Holy Spirit guide us through internal "promptings"?

9

today's session (cont'd)

are given peace with God. As we live our lives, the Spirit seeks to produce the peace of Christ in our hearts (Gal. 5:22).

<u>The second way we can sense the Spirit's guidance is through His work with our conscience.</u> Paul explains how this works in Romans 9:1–2, "I speak the truth in Christ—I am not lying, my conscience confirms it in the Holy Spirit—I have great sorrow and unceasing anguish in my heart." The Spirit will bring conviction when we sin, the truth of Scripture when we are faced with moral dilemmas, and godly knowledge when we don't know how to react or respond in certain situations.

notes:

✝

Remain in groups of 6–8 people, in a horseshoe configuration.

In this small-group session, students will be applying the lessons of the text to their own lives through the following questions.

The students were asked (in the student book) to choose an answer for each question and explain why.

Learning from the Story (5-7 minutes)

1. Describe a time recently when the Holy Spirit provided great encouragement and/or direction in your life.

2. In verse 7, Jesus told His disciples, "It is for your good that I am going away." How would Jesus' absence be beneficial to His disciples?

3. What is the greatest barrier you are currently facing in following the Spirit's guidance in your life?

   ☐ I'm too busy.
   ☐ I'm afraid He'll want me to do something I don't want to do.
   ☐ I'm not really expecting Him to communicate with me.
   ☐ I'm not doing something He's already told me to do.
   ☐ I'm too set in my ways.
   ☐ Other: _____

life change lessons (5-7 minutes)

Share with the class the following thoughts on how the lessons of this text might be applied today. The answers to the student book questions (provided in the margin) are underlined unless the question requires a personal answer.

Why is it often so difficult to hear God's voice during the daily routine of life?

What are three practical ways you can become more aware of the Spirit's "promptings" in your life?

The ability to discern the Holy Spirit's leading in your life often takes some effort. <u>Because you are used to hearing so many "voices" speaking to you every day, you must train your heart to be sensitive to the Spirit's voice.</u> For many people, their typical routine begins with reading the newspaper, listening to the radio during their commute to work, reading billboards along the road, and listening to the opinions of many who may not be walking with God. After arriving home, they spend an hour or so watching the news on television along with other television shows. You must train your heart to hear God's voice in the midst of all the other messages that come your way. Here are some practical ways to help you become more aware of the Spirit "promptings" in your life.

1. <u>PUT UP YOUR "SPIRITUAL ANTENNAS" EACH DAY AND LISTEN FOR THE SPIRIT'S "PROMPTINGS."</u> Many Christians miss out on being used by God in their daily routine simply because they are not listening for God to speak through His Spirit. Starting your mornings with meditation on God's Word and in prayer can focus your heart and tune your mind to hear God later in the day. Remember, God is not bound by your schedule or busy calendar. He speaks to you at any time. If you're too busy for God, then you're busier than God ever intended for you to be!

2. <u>KEEP A JOURNAL OF THE SPIRIT'S "PROMPTINGS" IN YOUR LIFE EACH DAY THIS WEEK.</u> One way to be more sensitive to the Spirit's leading in your life is to keep a daily journal of the times in your day that you believe the Spirit was prompting you. Maybe you sensed the Spirit leading you to encourage someone, help someone, or confront someone. Perhaps you sensed His peace as you contemplated a difficult decision you had to make. Maybe you felt His conviction concerning a sin you committed. Whatever it is, record those times each day this week. You may be surprised at how much the Spirit speaks to you each day.

3. <u>PRAY THAT GOD WILL GIVE YOU HIS PEACE IN THE CRITICAL DECISIONS YOU ARE FACING.</u> Are there any big or difficult decisions you will have to make within the next few weeks or month? If so, begin praying now that God will give you His peace about the right choice. In Philippians 4:6–7, we see this principle: "Do not be anxious about anything, but in everything, by prayer and petition, with thanksgiving, present your requests to God. And the peace of God, which transcends all understanding, will guard your hearts and your minds in Christ Jesus."

9

♘ CARING TIME
Remain in groups of 6–8 people, in a horseshoe configuration.

Hand out the Prayer/Praise Report to the entire group. Ask each subgroup to pray for the empty chair. Pray specifically for God to guide you to someone to bring next week to fill that chair.

After a sufficient time of prayer in subgroups, close in a corporate prayer. Say, "Next week we will talk about: 'Choosing to Grow in Faith.'"

Remind participants of the daily Scripture readings and reflective questions found on page 112.

Caring Time (15-20 minutes)

Use this time to pray for one another concerning the critical decisions you may be facing within the next few days, weeks, or months. Go around the group and have each person pray for the person on his or her right. Pray that God will help this group member overcome his or her greatest barrier to following the Holy Spirit's guidance as discussed in question 3 under "Learning from the Story." Start with this sentence:

"Dear God, I want to talk with you about my friend _____."

Close by asking God to replace any anxieties you are feeling with peace in the coming week, and by praying for the concerns listed on the Prayer/Praise Report.

notes:

BIBLE STUDY NOTES

JOHN 16:5
Jesus' teaching

Reference Notes

Use these notes to gain further understanding of the text as you study on your own.

none of you asks. Peter did ask this question in John 13:36: "Lord, where are you going?" and Jesus replied: "Where I am going, you cannot follow now, but you will follow later." Some commentators see this as evidence that chapters 13–16 are a compilation of several teachings of Jesus arranged in this format to give a summary of Jesus' teaching to believers. Others think that Jesus is responding to the fact that Peter didn't understand the significance of the answer Jesus gave to Peter's question.

✝

JOHN 16:7
the Counselor

It is for your good that I am going away. Jesus' departure meant the coming of the Counselor. The Greek term used for the Holy Spirit is *paraclete*. It is a rich term for which there is no adequate English translation. Attempts such as *Counselor* or *Helper* or *Comforter* fail because they emphasize only one of many aspects of the term. Jesus is telling the disciples that He will return to them in a deep, inner, spiritual way. He had also referred to the Spirit in John 7:38–39: "Whoever believes in me, as the Scripture has said, streams of living water will flow from within him." By this He meant the Spirit, whom those who believed in Him were later to receive. Up to that time the Spirit had not been given, since Jesus had not yet been glorified (see also John 14:15–18).

JOHN 16:8
conviction

he will convict the world of guilt in regard to sin and righteousness and judgment. The "world" held that Jesus was an unrighteous sinner under the judgment of God (John 9:24). The Spirit will prove that the world is wrong about its convictions on these matters. "Righteousness" (perhaps better translated as "justice") is shown by the Father's vindication of Jesus through His resurrection and ascension (v. 10).

JOHN 16:13
the Trinity

He will not speak on his own. Jesus only speaks the words of His Father; the Spirit only speaks the words of Jesus. Each member of the Trinity seeks the glory and honor of the other (see John 8:54; 12:28; 16:14; 17:1,4–5).

JOHN 16:15
the truth

All that belongs to the Father is mine ... the Spirit will ... make it known to you. The incredible truth of the gospel is that God has fully revealed Himself to His people. Even believers who never saw Jesus physically are not at a disadvantage compared to those who did, for the Spirit continually reveals Jesus and the Father to whomever comes in faith to Christ.

JOHN 16:16
spiritual sight

In a little while ... then after a little while. This riddle may be intentionally ambiguous. Does the first "little while" mean after His resurrection or after His return in glory? Does "seeing" mean physical sight or spiritual sight—as it so often does in this Gospel? If the latter, then the second "little while" may mean His coming to them by His Spirit (John 14:18–20). It would not be unlike this author to mean all the above!

9

notes:

[1] Bernard Ramm, *Protestant Biblical Interpretations*, 3rd Edition (Grand Rapids, MI: Baker Book House, 1970), 18.

Session

10

Choosing to Grow in Faith

Prepare for the Session

	READINGS	REFLECTIVE QUESTIONS
Monday	Genesis 45:4–5	Has someone close to you ever betrayed you? How did you respond?
Tuesday	Genesis 45:6–11	How has God met your needs unexpectedly within the past year?
Wednesday	Genesis 50:15	When have you held a grudge against someone? How did it make you feel?
Thursday	Genesis 50:16–17	Have you ever had difficulty forgiving someone who hurt or offended you?
Friday	Genesis 50:18–19	What "fear" can keep people from asking someone to forgive them?
Saturday	Genesis 50:20	How has God accomplished His purposes in your life through some of the adversity you've faced?
Sunday	Genesis 50:21	How do you think Joseph's brothers felt after hearing these words?

notes:

OUR GOALS FOR
THIS SESSION ARE:

⋃ **In groups of 6–8,
gather people in
a horseshoe
configuration.**

**Make sure everyone
has a name tag.**

**Take time to share
information on class
parties that are coming
up as well as any
relevant church events.**

✝

BIBLE STUDY	• to understand the way God uses circumstances in our lives
	• to learn how to face the difficult circumstances we encounter in life
	• to understand how Joseph continued to trust God and live for Him in adversity
LIFE CHANGE	• to spend time with those who have matured in their faith through adversity
	• to study the biblical stories of those who experienced great adversity, yet saw the will of God accomplished in their lives
	• to confess to God any bitterness we've allowed to creep into our lives because of the trials we've been through

Icebreaker (10-15 minutes)

**INTRODUCE THE
ICEBREAKER ACTIVITY:
The students have
been given instructions
in their books.**

**After the Icebreaker
say something like,
"Family reunions
can prove to be
very interesting
affairs, depending
on who shows up!
Today we'll study an
incredible family
reunion that shows
how God can work
through adversity."**

**Hand out the
Prayer/Praise Report.
A sample copy is
on pages 158-159.
Have people write
down prayer requests
and praises. Then
have the prayer
coordinator collect
the report and make
copies for use during
the Caring Time.**

Family Reunion. Which of the following persons would most likely show up at your family reunion?

☐ someone who was a contestant on *Who Wants to Be a Millionaire?*
☐ someone who's been to the Daytona 500
☐ someone who lived during the Great Depression
☐ someone who tried out for the television show *Survivor*
☐ someone who visits Graceland annually
☐ someone who always has an unbelievable story to tell
☐ someone who's shopped in Beverly Hills
☐ someone who still believes that pro wrestling is real
☐ someone who's always got an opinion about politics
☐ someone who ran in the Boston Marathon
☐ someone who could have been a cast member on *Cheers*

10

*n*otes:

✝

GENESIS 45:4–11

Have two members
of the class, selected
ahead of time, read
the passages from
Genesis. Have one
person read 45:4–11
and the other read
50:15–21.

50:15–21

Bible Study (30-45 minutes)

The Scripture for this week:

⁴Then Joseph said to his brothers, "Come close to me." When they had done so, he said, "I am your brother Joseph, the one you sold into Egypt! ⁵And now, do not be distressed and do not be angry with yourselves for selling me here, because it was to save lives that God sent me ahead of you. ⁶For two years now there has been famine in the land, and for the next five years there will not be plowing and reaping. ⁷But God sent me ahead of you to preserve for you a remnant on earth and to save your lives by a great deliverance.

⁸"So then, it was not you who sent me here, but God. He made me father to Pharaoh, lord of his entire household and ruler of all Egypt. ⁹Now hurry back to my father and say to him, 'This is what your son Joseph says: God has made me lord of all Egypt. Come down to me; don't delay. ¹⁰You shall live in the region of Goshen and be near me— you, your children and grandchildren, your flocks and herds, and all you have. ¹¹I will provide for you there, because five years of famine are still to come. Otherwise you and your household and all who belong to you will become destitute.' " ...

¹⁵When Joseph's brothers saw that their father was dead, they said, "What if Joseph holds a grudge against us and pays us back for all the wrongs we did to him?" ¹⁶So they sent word to Joseph, saying, "Your father left these instructions before he died: ¹⁷'This is what you are to say to Joseph: I ask you to forgive your brothers the sins and the wrongs they committed in treating you so badly.' Now please forgive the sins of the servants of the God of your father." When their message came to him, Joseph wept.

¹⁸His brothers then came and threw themselves down before him. "We are your slaves," they said.

¹⁹But Joseph said to them, "Don't be afraid. Am I in the place of God? ²⁰You intended to harm me, but God intended it for good to accomplish what is now being done, the saving of many lives. ²¹So then, don't be afraid. I will provide for you and your children." And he reassured them and spoke kindly to them.

notes:

Summarize these introductory remarks. Be sure to include the underlined information, which gives the answers to the student book questions (provided in the margin).

...about today's session (5 minutes)

RESPONDING TO GAME SITUATIONS

Successful football players are always aware of the score, yardage needed for a first down, and the amount of time remaining on the game clock. Their actions are often determined by these factors. For instance, a quarterback might throw the ball away to stop the clock, call time out to prevent a penalty if the play clock is about to run out, or call an audible at the line of scrimmage (to change the play because of the defensive alignment he sees).

What will your response to the circumstances of life determine?

In the same way, our response to the circumstances of life will determine our success in life. An obvious example of someone who fought through terrible loss and pain was Job. In the midst of tremendous blessing, he lost his family and everything he owned, including his health. At the end of those terrible tragedies, he discovered more blessing and purpose in his life than he had ever experienced. We see this in Job 42:12: "The Lord blessed the latter part of Job's life more than the first." The key was Job's response to his adversity. At the beginning, Job struggled with understanding why he was experiencing all of those difficult circumstances. However, in Job 42:1–6, Job comes to grips with God's sovereignty and learns to trust God's heart.

How did Job discover more blessing and purpose during the latter part of his life?

Then Job replied to the Lord:
  2"I know that you can do all things;
  no plan of yours can be thwarted.
3You asked, 'Who is this that obscures my counsel without
    knowledge?'
  Surely I spoke of things I did not understand,
  things too wonderful for me to know.
4"You said, 'Listen now, and I will speak;
  I will question you,
  and you shall answer me.'
5My ears had heard of you
  but now my eyes have seen you.
6Therefore I despise myself
  and repent in dust and ashes."

Job learned how to trust God in the midst of confusing and difficult circumstances. In today's session, we will look at another Old Testament character named Joseph. Joseph also learned how to relate to God during adverse circumstances in such a way that God's will was accomplished in his life.

10

☩

Identifying with the Story (5-7 minutes)

☋ Remain in groups of 6–8 people, in a horseshoe configuration.

In this small group session, students will be responding to the following questions that will help them share their stories in terms of Joseph's response when reunited with his family in Genesis 45:4–11 and 50:15–21.

Have the students explore these questions together.

1. What was your favorite place to eat when you were a child? Where is your favorite place to eat now?

2. Which of the following people would you most like to run into at the mall? Mark your answer with an **X**. Which of the following persons would you least like to run into at the mall? Mark your answer with a ✔.

   ☐ one of my high school teachers
   ☐ an old flame from high school
   ☐ a former neighbor
   ☐ someone from my place of employment
   ☐ a survey taker
   ☐ an ex-wife / ex-husband
   ☐ my best friend from elementary school
   ☐ other:_____

3. When you were a child, what were you most afraid of?

   ☐ the dark   ☐ my parents
   ☐ being alone   ☐ a teacher
   ☐ getting lost   ☐ the police
   ☐ the school bully   ☐ swimming
   ☐ other:_____

notes:

today's session (15-20 minutes)

Share with your class the following information which you may modify according to your own perspectives and teaching needs. The answers to the student book questions (provided in the margin) are underlined.

Charles Swindoll said, "I am convinced that life is ___% what happens to me and ___% how I react to it."

In today's session, we will learn the value of trusting God even in the face of difficult circumstances. When faced with adversity, we can easily get disillusioned concerning God's presence and faithfulness in our lives. The way we respond to our circumstances will determine how well we fulfill God's purposes for our lives. Charles Swindoll said, "I am convinced that life is 10% what happens to me and 90% how I react to it."[1] Some people respond to adverse situations with a negative attitude. Others, like these campers, respond with a positive attitude.

> A bounty of $5,000 was offered for each wolf captured alive. Sam and Jed saw dollar signs so they became overnight bounty hunters. They scoured the mountains both day and night in search of their fortune. After several days of unsuccessful hunting, they fell asleep from exhaustion. In the middle of the night, Sam suddenly awoke to see that they were surrounded by about fifty wolves with flaming eyes and bared teeth. He nudged his partner, "Jed, wake up! We're rich!"[2]

What are some ways God uses circumstances to get our attention?

God wants to use the circumstances that come our way in life in several ways. The first way God uses circumstances is to get our attention. God may get our attention through the words of another person, the way He answers our prayers, the amount of time He takes to answer our prayers, pain or sickness, blessings, tragedy, financial collapse in the economy, failure, war, disappointment, and anything else He chooses. God uses different methods at different times with different people. In the life of King David, God used the words of Nathan the prophet, a spokesman for God, to grab David's attention so he would hear from God (2 Sam. 12:1–13). When Balaam headed out in the wrong direction, God got his attention by speaking through the donkey he was riding (see Num. 22:21–34)!

How does God use circumstances to gain our affection?

The second way God uses circumstances is to gain our affection. God's faithfulness in adversity draws us to our Father's side in love and adoration. As we learn to depend on God during trying times, we grow in our love for God (see Rom. 5:3–5).

10

How does God use circumstances to grow our character?

The third way God uses circumstances is to grow our character. Ron Dunn writes, "To God character is far more precious than comfort. He often uses uncomfortable circumstances to change our character. When the circumstances have fulfilled their task, then God may change the circumstances. But if he doesn't, it will be all right because our character will have been so changed that we will be able to live with uncomfortable circumstances."[3] Paul was confident that "suffering produces perseverance; perseverance, character" (Rom. 5:3–4).

today's session (cont'd)

In our story today, we discover several principles from Joseph's life that will help us respond to the difficult circumstances we face in life. Joseph was well acquainted with adversity. His brothers sold him into slavery because they were jealous of the attention he was receiving from their father and because they were angry with him over his dreams that depicted his family bowing to him (see Gen. 37). Potiphar's wife falsely accused him of rape. He was thrown into prison and then was forgotten by the chief cupbearer whom he had helped. Through God's favor and Joseph's commitment to serving the Lord God, Joseph was eventually elevated to second-in-charge over all of Egypt. We pick up the story with Joseph revealing his true identity to his brothers. In verse 4, Joseph drops the "bombshell": "I am your brother Joseph, the one you sold into Egypt!"

What are three ways Joseph successfully dealt with the difficult circumstances he faced?

Joseph could have blamed his brothers for all the trouble he had encountered, but he didn't. <u>The first way Joseph dealt with his difficult circumstances was by refusing to blame others</u>. When things turn out bad, we often want to find a reason outside of ourselves. Joseph knew that placing blame would not improve his situation. Instead, he saw God's fingerprints over the unfortunate circumstances that had come his way: "God sent me ahead of you to preserve for you a remnant on earth and to save your lives by a great deliverance" (Gen. 45:7). In Genesis 45:5, Joseph reassures his brothers with these words, "Do not be distressed and do not be angry with yourselves for selling me here, because it was to save lives that God sent me ahead of you."

<u>The second way Joseph kept the right outlook on his circumstances was by resisting the grip of bitterness</u>. In Genesis 50:15, this was a concern of his brothers: " 'What if Joseph holds a grudge against us and pays us back for all the wrongs we did to him?' " They knew that what they had done was wrong—and they knew how they would have responded! Bitterness can emerge in our lives if we only focus on the "snapshots" of the circumstances. Joseph chose to trust God with all the "snapshots" of his life and how they fit into God's big picture. Sometimes we won't understand how they all fit together until we enter God's presence in eternity. Joseph, however, saw first hand that God was using his difficult circumstances for a greater good, and he refused to become bitter toward his brothers: " 'Don't be afraid. I will provide for you and your children.' And he reassured them and spoke kindly to them" (Gen. 50:21).

<u>The third way Joseph stayed in the will of God was by recognizing that God's timing was perfect</u>. Our ability to interpret our circumstances is very limited. In Genesis 50:20, we see that Joseph trusted

God's timing: "You intended to harm me, but God intended it for good to accomplish what is now being done, the saving of many lives."

Throughout his trials, Joseph continued to trust God and live for Him, making right decisions in the critical moments of his life. Joseph submitted to God in every area of his life. He was honorable and faithful to God during his years of slavery and imprisonment. Through it all, he never lost hope in God. Joseph learned a valuable lesson: God is always at work, even in the darkness. God has a purpose for all the circumstances we face in life, whether good or bad. In Romans 8:28, Paul writes, "We know that in all things God works for the good of those who love him, who have been called according to his purpose."

notes:

10

♘ Remain in groups
of 6–8 people, in
a horseshoe
configuration.

In this small-group
session, students will
be applying the lessons
of the text to their
own lives through the
following questions.

The students were
asked (in the student
book) to choose an
answer for each
question and
explain why.

Learning from the Story (5-7 minutes)

1. If you had been in Joseph's shoes, what would you have done when your brothers asked for food during the famine?

2. Of the things that Joseph said to his brothers, which do you think was the most surprising statement the brothers heard?

   ☐ "Come close to me."
   ☐ "I am your brother Joseph, the one you sold into Egypt."
   ☐ "God sent me ... to save your lives."
   ☐ "It was not you who sent me here, but God."
   ☐ "He [God] made me ... ruler of all Egypt."
   ☐ "Don't be afraid."
   ☐ "I will provide for you and your children."

3. How do you react when someone asks you to forgive him or her?

   ☐ On the surface I act fine, but on the inside I question the person's sincerity.
   ☐ I act like everything's all right, but I still hold a grudge.
   ☐ I tell him or her that it's no big deal and everyone makes mistakes.
   ☐ I wouldn't know because those who have hurt or offended me have never asked.
   ☐ I forgive the person instantly because I know that Christ has forgiven me.
   ☐ I apologize also, even though I didn't do anything wrong.
   ☐ Other:_____

notes:

Share with the class the following thoughts on how the lessons of this text might be applied today. The answers to the student book questions (provided in the margin) are underlined unless the question requires a personal answer.

What does Matthew 5:45 tell you about adversity?

What are three steps you can take that will help you respond to the difficult circumstances of life?

life change lessons (5-7 minutes)

All of us will go through the school of hard knocks. In Matthew 5:45, Jesus said, "He [God] causes his sun to rise on the evil and the good, and sends rain on the righteous and the unrighteous." Christians are certainly not exempt from experiencing difficult circumstances. Your response to them should reflect your trust in God and His wisdom and love for you. Here are steps you can take to prepare your heart for responding to the difficult circumstances of life:

1. SPEND TIME WITH THOSE WHO HAVE GROWN IN THEIR FAITH THROUGH ADVERSITY. Life's best lessons are those that are experienced. You can learn a great deal by spending time with those who have grown in their faith through difficult circumstances. Ask what they struggled with and how they persevered during their trials.

2. STUDY THE BIBLICAL STORIES OF THOSE WHO EXPERIENCED GREAT ADVERSITY, YET SAW THE WILL OF GOD ACCOMPLISHED IN THEIR LIVES. In Romans 15:4, we learn that "everything that was written in the past was written to teach us, so that through endurance and the encouragement of the Scriptures we might have hope." Some of the biblical characters that endured great adversity and then experienced God's will being achieved in their lives include Moses, David, Paul, and Jesus.

3. CONFESS TO GOD ANY BITTERNESS YOU'VE ALLOWED TO CREEP INTO YOUR LIFE BECAUSE OF THE TRIALS YOU'VE BEEN THROUGH. The trials you face are not meant to build a wall between God and you or other Christians. They are meant to build your character, get your attention, or gain your affection. Bitterness comes from turning your questions and anger inward. It destroys your love and trust in God. In Ephesians 4:31, Paul instructs us to: "Get rid of all bitterness, rage and anger." It's your choice—you can choose to get bitter or get better.

notes:

10

CARING TIME

Remain in groups of 6–8 people, in a horseshoe configuration.

Hand out the Prayer/ Praise Report to the entire group. Ask each subgroup to pray for the empty chair. Pray specifically for God to guide you to someone to bring next week to fill that chair.

After a sufficient time of prayer in subgroups, close in a corporate prayer. Say, "Next week we will talk about 'Choosing Godly Counsel.' "

Remind participants of the daily Scripture readings and reflective questions found on page 124.

Caring Time   (15-20 minutes)

Close by sharing prayer requests and praying for one another. Have group members share any difficult circumstances they are going through right now. Pray that they will trust God through it all. In addition, pray for the concerns on the Prayer/Praise Report.

notes:

BIBLE STUDY NOTES

GENESIS 45:4
power

GENESIS 45:5
God's sovereign control

Reference Notes

Use these notes to gain further understanding
of the text as you study on your own.

I am your brother Joseph. Joseph's brothers were terrified of their brother whom they had sold into slavery (see Gen. 37:28). Joseph had the power to exact revenge on them because of their betrayal if he chose to do so.

God sent me. God was working behind the scenes to carry out His purposes, namely to preserve the nation of Israel during the famine. God used Joseph as His chosen instrument in the palace of the pharaoh. God would not allow the evil actions of people to dictate his plan. Instead, we see God's sovereign control in human affairs.

GENESIS 45:7

a remnant. God would not allow His chosen people, Israel, to die because of the famine.

GENESIS 45:8

father. This was a title of honor given to high officials in Egypt.

lord ... ruler. Joseph's power was almost absolute; in Egypt, he was second only to pharaoh.

GENESIS 50:17

Joseph wept. Joseph was both emotional and sensitive (see Gen. 42:24; 43:30; 45:2,14–15; 46:29).

GENESIS 50:18

threw themselves down. This was a fulfillment of Joseph's earlier dreams (see Gen. 37:7,9).

GENESIS 50:19
revenge

Am I in the place of God? Joseph wanted his brothers to know that he wasn't interested in playing God by seeking revenge on them. Joseph knew that God was the only One who could deal with injustices.

GENESIS 50:20
God's purpose

God used the evil treatment of Joseph's brothers, being falsely accused by Potiphar's wife, and being forgotten in prison, to achieve His purpose. When we trust God during difficult times, He is faithful to work good from it.

God intended it for good. On the surface, what Joseph's brothers did to him was a terrible act. Behind the scenes, however, God was making sure Joseph was in the right position to carry out His greater plan—to save the lives of the people of Israel and the other nations who came to buy food during the famine.

notes:

10

[1] Raymond McHenry, ed., *The Best of In Other Words* (Houston, TX: Raymond McHenry, 1996), 49.

[2] Ibid., 324.

[3] Ron Dunn, *Will God Heal Me?* (Sisters, OR: Multnomah, 1997), 168.

Session

11

Choosing Godly Counsel

Prepare for the Session

	READINGS	REFLECTIVE QUESTIONS
Monday	1 Kings 12:1–4	As a leader, are you more of a servant or a taskmaster?
Tuesday	1 Kings 12:5	How long do you usually take before making a major decision?
Wednesday	1 Kings 12:6–11	Where do you typically go for advice?
Thursday	1 Kings 12:12–14	When have you let worldly counsel replace godly counsel? What was the result?
Friday	Proverbs 15:22	What is the key to making good plans and decisions?
Saturday	Proverbs 3:7	Why do you think many people don't seek wise counsel?
Sunday	Proverbs 12:15	What is one characteristic of a wise person? Do you have this characteristic?

notes:

✝

OUR GOALS FOR THIS SESSION ARE:

⊌ **In groups of 6–8, gather people in a horseshoe configuration.**

Make sure everyone has a name tag.

Take time to share information on class parties that are coming up as well as any relevant church events.

INTRODUCE THE ICEBREAKER ACTIVITY: The students have been given instructions in their books.

After the Icebreaker say something like, "Most of the time it's a lot easier to give advice than to take it. We like to believe we have the wisdom to handle life on our own. Today we will look at the importance of seeking and following godly counsel."

Hand out the Prayer/Praise Report. A sample copy is on pages 158-159. Have people write down prayer requests and praises. Then have the prayer coordinator collect the report and make copies for use during the Caring Time.

BIBLE STUDY	• to understand the importance of seeking godly counsel
	• to learn how to identify those we should go to for counsel
	• to learn some effective questions to ask when seeking counsel
LIFE CHANGE	• to identify several individuals to whom we can go for godly counsel
	• to ask good questions when seeking godly counsel
	• to be open to God speaking to us through the counsel of others

Icebreaker (10-15 minutes)

Advice Column. You have been given the task of writing a weekly advice column in the church newsletter. Which of the following questions collected from church members would you choose to answer and put in the bulletin next Sunday? What advice would you give?

☐ "Why should I tithe? The church has enough money as it is."

☐ "Since I'm a faithful member, could the church designate a reserved parking space with my name on it that is close to the front door? What should I do first to get this done?"

☐ "Do I have to wear a suit and tie to church every Sunday?" —the Pastor

☐ "I'm a parent who is worried about my teenage son who talks about school shootings all the time. What should I do?"

☐ "I think my parents are about to get a divorce. I'm only 10 years old. What should I do?"

notes:

11

**LEARNING FROM
THE BIBLE**

1 KINGS 12:1–14

Have two members
of the class, selected
ahead of time, read
the passage from
1 Kings. Have one
person read the part
of Rehoboam and the
other read the rest of
the verses. Ask the
whole class to read
verse 4 together.

Bible Study (30-45 minutes)

The Scripture for this week:

¹*Rehoboam went to Shechem, for all the Israelites had gone there to make him king.* ²*When Jeroboam son of Nebat heard this (he was still in Egypt, where he had fled from King Solomon), he returned from Egypt.* ³*So they sent for Jeroboam, and he and the whole assembly of Israel went to Rehoboam and said to him:* ⁴*"Your father put a heavy yoke on us, but now lighten the harsh labor and the heavy yoke he put on us, and we will serve you."*

⁵*Rehoboam answered, "Go away for three days and then come back to me." So the people went away.*

⁶*Then King Rehoboam consulted the elders who had served his father Solomon during his lifetime. "How would you advise me to answer these people?" he asked.*

⁷*They replied, "If today you will be a servant to these people and serve them and give them a favorable answer, they will always be your servants."*

⁸*But Rehoboam rejected the advice the elders gave him and consulted the young men who had grown up with him and were serving him.* ⁹*He asked them, "What is your advice? How should we answer these people who say to me, 'Lighten the yoke your father put on us'?"*

¹⁰*The young men who had grown up with him replied, "Tell these people who have said to you, 'Your father put a heavy yoke on us, but make our yoke lighter'—tell them, 'My little finger is thicker than my father's waist.* ¹¹*My father laid on you a heavy yoke; I will make it even heavier. My father scourged you with whips; I will scourge you with scorpions.' "*

¹²*Three days later Jeroboam and all the people returned to Rehoboam, as the king had said, "Come back to me in three days."* ¹³*The king answered the people harshly. Rejecting the advice given him by the elders,* ¹⁴*he followed the advice of the young men and said, "My father made your yoke heavy; I will make it even heavier. My father scourged you with whips; I will scourge you with scorpions."*

notes:

Summarize these introductory remarks. Be sure to include the underlined information, which gives the answers to the student book questions (provided in the margin).

What life lesson can we learn from watching football players get in the huddle before each play?

What are some ways people seek counsel in our society?

...about today's session (5 minutes)

GETTING IN THE HUDDLE

Most professional football players have great individual skills that make them successful at what they do. Although they possess great strength, agility, and speed, there's still one thing those 11 guys do before almost every play—they huddle up! They get together and hear the upcoming play so they can all be on the same page when the ball is snapped. There is a great lesson for life to be learned by watching the huddle. <u>If players of great skill need to huddle up and hear instructions for each play, we also need the benefit of huddling up with others to receive wise instructions before following through on the critical decisions in our lives.</u> Proverbs 20:18 instructs us to, "Make plans by seeking advice."

The desire for wise counsel is an obvious need in society, evidenced by the many late night psychic infomercials. They wouldn't keep running the commercials if people weren't calling. <u>People are also looking to Internet chat rooms, fortune-tellers, numerologists, palm readers, or "Dear Abby" for advice.</u> They are looking for counsel in all the wrong places! In today's session, we will learn the importance of seeking godly counsel, counsel from people who love and fear God, people who know and live biblical directives. We will also seek to understand who qualifies as a godly counselor and some questions to ask when we meet with that person.

notes:

⟳ Remain in groups of 6–8 people, in a horseshoe configuration.

In this small group session, students will be responding to the following questions that will help them share their stories in terms of King Rehoboam's decision in 1 Kings 12:1–14.

Have the students explore these questions together.

✝

Identifying with the Story (5-7 minutes)

1. When you were a child and needed advice, where did you go? Has that changed now that you are older?

2. When you were a teenager, did you ever go against your parent's advice even though you knew you were wrong? What happened?

11

✝

Identifying with the Story (cont'd)

3. When you are faced with a big decision, how do you usually come up with your final course of action?

☐ I follow my gut reaction.

☐ I do a lot of research and analysis.

☐ I try to think of what my parents would do in a similar situation.

☐ I base it on my past experiences.

☐ I look to see what everyone else is doing and follow suit.

☐ I ask the opinions of those I feel are wiser or more experienced than I am.

☐ Other: _____

notes:

today's session (15-20 minutes)

Share with your class the following information which you may modify according to your own perspectives and teaching needs. The answers to the student book questions (provided in the margin) are underlined.

According to the leader, what is one reason many people get stressed out when making decisions?

What are three reasons people don't seek counsel when making decisions?

Many people get stressed out over some of the decisions they have to make in life. Those who experience great anxiety are most likely those who try to make decisions by themselves, based on their own experiences and knowledge. The problem with this is that our experience and knowledge are limited, like these visitors to Miami:

> Two men came to Miami from the Arctic regions where they had lived all their life. On the bus to the hotel they passed one of the bays where some people were water-skiing. Having seen only their kayaks and other hand-propelled boats throughout their lifetime, one man asked the other, "What makes that boat go so fast?" The other man watched for a few seconds, then replied, "Man on string push it."[1]

God has not designed us to make decisions independently or with limited information. Unfortunately, many Christians avoid seeking counsel from others during the critical decisions in life. There are several reasons why people don't seek outside counsel. Some individuals think they don't know anyone who could help them with important decisions. Another reason is pride. For some individuals, asking others for counsel is a sign of weakness. This is especially true of people in leadership roles. They may think that making decisions

128

based on their own intuition is what is expected of them. Great leaders have learned the importance of surrounding themselves with wise people and listening to their counsel. Great leadership does not mean a person makes decisions on his or her own. A mark of a great leader is owning the decision once it's been made. Another reason why godly counsel is avoided is that the person already knows what the answer will be and doesn't want to hear it. Even the wisest man who ever lived understood the importance of being surrounded with those who give godly counsel. In Proverbs 13:20, Solomon wrote: "He who walks with the wise grows wise, but a companion of fools suffers harm."

Why is seeking godly counsel a good idea?

We need to see that one benefit believers have is their place in the body of Christ where they can learn from one another and help each other make wise decisions. We can seek the wisdom of godly people who can help us see what we can't see from our point of view. One of the primary tools God uses to guide us is the counsel of other believers. Here are two reasons why seeking godly counsel is a good idea. First, we need wise, godly counsel because we lack objectivity. We tend to look at situations from our own viewpoint. If a situation is close to us, we need the help of others who can see the blind spots we can't. This is especially true in decisions involving relationships with friends and family, because they tend to involve our emotions and emotions sometimes cloud our vision. Second, seeking godly counsel is needed when we don't have enough information. It's also needed when making business or financial decisions outside our realm of knowledge. The complexity of the decision may be over our heads.

In today's Bible study, we'll pull out some principles that will help us utilize wise counsel in our daily decision making. In 1 Kings 12, we find Rehoboam being crowned king of Israel. During the coronation festivities, Jeroboam and the whole assembly of Israel plead for him to lighten the burden of taxes and the conscription of labor. They say to Rehoboam, " 'Your father put a heavy yoke on us, but now lighten the harsh labor and the heavy yoke he put on us, and we will serve you' " (1 Kings 12:4). He considers the request and decides to heed the advice of his friends and associates, rather than his father's older and wiser advisers. How can we make sure that we choose the right advisers?

What are some characteristics of the people we should seek for counsel?

Here are some characteristics of the kind of counsel we should seek. First, make sure it is someone who has nothing to lose by telling us the truth. We need to seek out those who are more concerned about telling us the truth than they are about preserving the friendship. Truth must always take precedent over preserving the relationship. Proverbs 27:5 says, "Better is open rebuke than hidden love."

11

today's session (cont'd)

Rehoboam sought advice from his friends and associates whose positions could be eliminated if the taxes and labor were lessened. Second, we should seek out someone who is where we want to be in life. We may seek the counsel of those who have experienced success in marriage, relationships, finances, and spiritual growth. The problem for many that are seeking good advice is they ask people who are no farther down the road than they are. Rehoboam should have listened to the older and wiser advisers who served his father, rather than those who were in the same situation he was in. Third, it is wise to ask more than one person if possible. Proverbs 15:22 says, "Plans fail for lack of counsel, but with many advisers they succeed." Rehoboam sought counsel from two different groups but chose to serve his own interests instead of the people under his leadership. Fourth, it can also prove beneficial to choose someone you know and someone you don't. This will likely insure a balance to the advice you will receive.

What are two good questions to ask when seeking counsel from others?

As we share our situation with a godly counselor, asking the right questions becomes very important. One question you can ask is, "Are any of the options I'm considering unscriptural?" Because it's easy to put our own spin on certain Scriptures for our benefit, letting others help us keep God's Word in its context is invaluable. This is also a good question for those who are relatively new believers and aren't sure what the Bible says about a situation. An additional question to ask is, "What do you think is the wisest thing for me to do?" Not every situation will have a clear right or wrong answer. Those from whom we are seeking counsel need to know all the facts and variables of the situation, so they can give some solid advice. Here's one warning about seeking counsel: Expect to hear from God when seeking godly counsel, but be careful not to take everything you hear as God speaking. In other words, don't put undue pressure on the person to speak on God's behalf. It is important to seek counsel from several individuals, not just one. Some great places to look include parents, pastors, and spiritually mature believers. Trust God to show you His will concerning the decisions you are making. Often, He reveals what we're looking for through the wise counsel of others.

notes:

✝

⚙ Remain in groups of 6–8 people, in a horseshoe configuration.

In this small-group session, students will be applying the lessons of the text to their own lives through the following questions.

The students were asked (in the student book) to choose an answer for each question and explain why.

Learning from the Story (5-7 minutes)

1. What were the elders really advising Rehoboam to do?

   ☐ make a good first impression
   ☐ treat the people better than his father Solomon had
   ☐ show the people he cared
   ☐ do something nice to win the loyalty of the people

2. Had you been around at the time, what advice would you have given Rehoboam? What would you have told him in order to convince him to follow your advice?

3. Which of the following reasons would most closely resemble the one you might use for not listening to the advice of someone older than you?

   ☐ I don't want to hear a lecture on how tough it was when they were young.
   ☐ I don't want to appear helpless.
   ☐ Older people look down on younger people.
   ☐ Society has changed since they were my age. They wouldn't understand.
   ☐ I already know what they'll say, so I'm not going to ask.
   ☐ I don't have any relationships with older people whom I would consider wise.
   ☐ I wouldn't think twice about asking an older person for advice.

4. Is there a critical decision you are facing right now? If so, seek the advice of your subgroup.

life change lessons (5-7 minutes)

Share with the class the following thoughts on how the lessons of this text might be applied today. The answers to the student book questions (provided in the margin) are underlined unless the question requires a personal answer.

The President of the United States has cabinet members. A CEO has board members. A head football coach has assistant coaches. Who do you have? In this age of gated communities and hurried lives, you can easily pass off this important tool God has given you for discerning His will and hearing Him speak to you. As situations change, those you go to for counsel may change. The important thing is that you be patient and take the time needed to listen to godly counsel. Here are some steps for getting started:

11

life change lessons (cont'd)

Name some individuals you could go to for godly counsel.

1. IDENTIFY SEVERAL INDIVIDUALS YOU CAN GO TO FOR GODLY COUNSEL. Wise counsel often comes from those whom God has placed in authority over you such as parents and pastors. Those who are older and more spiritually mature than you also should be considered. All that remains is to take the necessary time to meet with these individuals and learn all you can concerning the decisions you are facing.

2. ASK GOOD QUESTIONS WHEN SEEKING GODLY COUNSEL. You should ask those wise individuals if they know of any Scripture that pertains to your situation. You can also ask them what they think a wise decision would be based on your situation where no clear right and wrong is evident. If someone tells you to do something, you should always seek to understand the basis of his or her suggestion—and not pass responsibility for a decision on to someone else. Another great question is, "Have you ever faced a similar situation and how did it turn out?" This actually gives context to the advice you receive from that person. It's one thing to hear advice, it's another thing to receive godly counsel based on Scripture and personal experience.

What is an indication that you may not be open to God speaking to you through others?

3. BE OPEN TO GOD SPEAKING TO YOU THROUGH THE COUNSEL OF OTHERS. <u>If the only counsel you ever heed is that which agrees with what you already think, you may not be as open as you should be to God speaking through others</u>. Sometimes, the consensus of counsel you receive from others will be directly opposite to what you think. In those moments, you need to be especially open to the possibility that God may be trying to tell you something.

⚙ **CARING TIME**
Remain in groups of 6–8 people, in a horseshoe configuration.

notes:

Hand out the Prayer/Praise Report to the entire group. Ask each subgroup to pray for the empty chair. Pray specifically for God to guide you to someone to bring next week to fill that chair.

 Caring Time (15-20 minutes)

Pray for one another concerning the critical decisions that were mentioned in question 4 under "Learning from the Story." Also, use the Prayer/Praise Report and pray for the concerns listed.

After a sufficient time of prayer in subgroups, close in a corporate prayer. Say, "Next week we will talk about: 'Choosing God's Wisdom.'"

Close by thanking God for bringing you together as a group and by asking Him to provide each group member with many godly counselors.

BIBLE STUDY NOTES

Reference Notes

Use these notes to gain further understanding
of the text as you study on your own.

1 KINGS 12:1
Mosaic Law

Shechem. Located about 35 miles north of Jerusalem. This was a significant city in Israel's history. For example, this is where the Israelites dedicated themselves to keeping the Mosaic Law (Josh. 24:1–27). After Israel divided into two kingdoms, Shechem became the capital of the northern kingdom for a short period (1 Kings 12:25).

1 KINGS 12:2–5
taxation

Israel wanted Jeroboam to convey their concerns over labor and taxation before Rehoboam. The prophet Ahijah had already told Jeroboam that he would eventually rule 10 of the tribes after the kingdom divided. Jeroboam apparently didn't try to press the issue but, instead, let events play out naturally.

1 KINGS 12:6

the elders. Rehoboam sought input from those who had served as his father's official advisers. These elders were most likely the same age as Solomon.

1 KINGS 12:7

If today you will be a servant. Great leaders in God's economy are those who have a servant's heart like Jesus'.

1 KINGS 12:8

young men. Rehoboam assembled some of his own friends and associates for advice. Apparently, they were already serving him in some official capacity.

1 KINGS 12:10

My little finger is thicker than my father's waist. This hyperbole meant that the least severe treatment by Rehoboam would be far greater than his father's most oppressive measures.

1 KINGS 12:11

scorpions. These were leather lashes with sharp pieces of metal attached to them; it was a cruel whip used during this time.

1 KINGS 12:12–14
burden

Rather than listening to the elder's advice, Rehoboam decided to serve his own interests and actually increase the burden on the people. This decision would contribute to the eventual division of the kingdom into two separate kingdoms.

notes:

11

¹ James S. Hewitt, ed., *Illustrations Unlimited* (Wheaton, IL: Tyndale House, 1988), 414.

Session

12

Choosing God's Wisdom

Prepare for the Session

	READINGS	REFLECTIVE QUESTIONS
Monday	James 1:1–2	How do you usually respond to adversity?
Tuesday	James 1:3–4	How has adversity strengthened your faith in God?
Wednesday	James 1:5	When you lack wisdom, who do you usually go to for wisdom?
Thursday	James 1:6	Is there any difficulty in your life that you doubt God can help you with?
Friday	James 1:7–8	Why do you think God would not entrust a double-minded person with His answers to prayer?
Saturday	James 1:9–11	In what ways do you need God's perspective on your financial situation?
Sunday	James 1:12	How does your love for God help you endure trials?

notes:

OUR GOALS FOR THIS SESSION ARE:

⋃ **In groups of 6–8, gather people in a horseshoe configuration.**

Make sure everyone has a name tag.

Take time to share information on class parties that are coming up as well as any relevant church events.

INTRODUCE THE ICEBREAKER ACTIVITY: The students have been given instructions in their books.

After the Icebreaker say something like, "We all experience times of adversity, but our individual reactions to it are quite varied. Today we will talk about keeping our joy during the trials of life by relying on God's wisdom."

Hand out the Prayer/Praise Report. A sample copy is on pages 158-159. Have people write down prayer requests and praises. Then have the prayer coordinator collect the report and make copies for use during the Caring Time.

✝ BIBLE STUDY · to learn why we need God's wisdom to handle adversity
· to understand the importance of fully trusting in God for wisdom
· to understand how relying on God's wisdom changes our focus

LIFE CHANGE · to stop trusting in worldly wisdom
· to start asking for the wisdom of God
· to learn the wisdom that God has already given you in His Word

Icebreaker   (10-15 minutes)

Joy Meter. Which one of the following common difficulties have you experienced most recently? Place an "X" on the scale below, indicating the amount of joy you kept in the midst of your adversity.

I HAD A BAD HAIR DAY
I lost my joy · · · · · · · · · I kept my joy

 I GOT A SPEEDING TICKET
I lost my joy · · · · · · · · · I kept my joy

MY FAVORITE TEAM LOST
I lost my joy · · · · · · · · · I kept my joy

MY STOCK VALUES DROPPED
I lost my joy · · · · · · · · · I kept my joy

 I HAD AN ARGUMENT
I lost my joy · · · · · · · · · I kept my joy

 I GOT STUCK IN A TRAFFIC JAM
I lost my joy · · · · · · · · · I kept my joy

 I HAD CAR PROBLEMS
I lost my joy · · · · · · · · · I kept my joy

 AN UNEXPECTED EXPENSE CAME UP
I lost my joy · · · · · · · · · I kept my joy

12

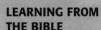

**LEARNING FROM
THE BIBLE**

JAMES 1:1–12

**Have a member of
the class, selected
ahead of time, read
the passage from
James.**

Bible Study   (30-45 minutes)

The Scripture for this week:

¹*James, a servant of God and of the Lord Jesus Christ, To the twelve tribes scattered among the nations: Greetings.*

²*Consider it pure joy, my brothers, whenever you face trials of many kinds, ³because you know that the testing of your faith develops perseverance. ⁴Perseverance must finish its work so that you may be mature and complete, not lacking anything. ⁵If any of you lacks wisdom, he should ask God, who gives generously to all without finding fault, and it will be given to him. ⁶But when he asks, he must believe and not doubt, because he who doubts is like a wave of the sea, blown and tossed by the wind. ⁷That man should not think he will receive anything from the Lord; ⁸he is a double-minded man, unstable in all he does.*

⁹*The brother in humble circumstances ought to take pride in his high position. ¹⁰But the one who is rich should take pride in his low position, because he will pass away like a wild flower. ¹¹For the sun rises with scorching heat and withers the plant; its blossom falls and its beauty is destroyed. In the same way, the rich man will fade away even while he goes about his business.*

¹²*Blessed is the man who perseveres under trial, because when he has stood the test, he will receive the crown of life that God has promised to those who love him.*

notes:

Summarize these introductory remarks. Be sure to include the underlined information, which gives the answers to the student book questions (provided in the margin).

...about today's session (5 minutes)

ASKING THE COACH

There are times in a football game where the quarterback calls a time-out to talk things over with his head coach. Maybe the opposing defense was not what he was anticipating. Maybe he was not confident in the play he was about to run. In the same way, there are times in our lives when we will not know what choice we should make or how we should respond in a particular time of adversity. In those times, we can gain valuable insight by taking a time out to ask our heavenly "Head Coach" for wisdom.

In 1 Kings 3:9–14, what did Solomon request from God?

What else did God grant Solomon, showing how pleased He was with Solomon's request?

In the Old Testament, there's a tremendous story of how King Solomon received great wisdom to rule Israel. Solomon knew that the job of king was too big for him to fulfill adequately. Solomon's request for <u>wisdom</u> (1 Kings 3:9–14) pleased God so much that Solomon not only received unequalled wisdom, <u>but God also gave him riches and honor above all other kings in the world</u>. We still have evidence of this wisdom in the Old Testament book of Proverbs. We can still gain insight from the wisdom that God bestowed on Solomon by reading it on a regular basis. When we ask God for wisdom we can be sure that He will be pleased (1 Kings 3:10). We may not receive the riches and honor of a king, but we will gain greater riches that will last an eternity.

In this session, we will look at how our search for wisdom arises out of the trials of life. We will also look at how to ask for God's wisdom. We will then see how God's wisdom changes our focus in the midst of life's ups and downs. Above all, we will seek to increase our faith in God during the times when we have every inclination to question God's power and purpose in our lives.

notes:

12

137

Remain in groups of 6–8 people, in a horseshoe configuration.

In this small group session, students will be responding to the following questions that will help them share their stories in terms of James' words about trials and wisdom in James 1:1–12.

Have the students explore these questions together.

Identifying with the Story (5-7 minutes)

1. Which one of the following movie titles most clearly describes a difficult trial you've experienced recently?

   ☐ *The Perfect Storm*
   ☐ *Dumb and Dumber*
   ☐ *Tourist Trap*
   ☐ *The Money Pit*
   ☐ *Meet the Parents*
   ☐ *Animal House*
   ☐ *Jaws*
   ☐ Other: _____

2. During your high school years, which one of the following phrases describes the approach you held regarding taking tests?

   ☐ "It was like throwing darts blindfolded."
   ☐ "Study hard and play hard."
   ☐ "Love thy neighbor's answers as thy own."
   ☐ "What test? I didn't know there was a test today."
   ☐ "Let's see, if I make a 50, that will get a C in the class; if I make a 60, that will get me a B in the class; if I make a … ."
   ☐ "Everything came pretty easy for me. I didn't have to cram much at all."
   ☐ Other: _____

3. In our Scripture passage today, James compares the person who doubts with "a wave of the sea, blown and tossed by the wind" (v. 6). Describe the worst weather event you've been through and how you responded to it.

notes:

Share with your class the following information which you may modify according to your own perspectives and teaching needs. The answers to the student book questions (provided in the margin) are underlined.

What "required course" do all believers have to take in this life?

In John 16:32–33, how did Jesus prepare His disciples for the trials they would encounter?

What are three reasons we need God's wisdom for handling adversity?

today's session (15-20 minutes)

When high school graduates are accepted into college and plan the courses they will take, they must first sign up for the core curriculum. These classes are mandatory for all students and are designed to form a solid foundation on which to build their major. In the same way, as we are accepted into God's family through faith, we sign up for God's core curriculum. Every believer experiences adversity in life. The trials of life are a required course. No one is exempt. God knows that through the testing of our faith, we will develop a solid foundation on which to build spiritual maturity. In John 16:32–33, Jesus told His disciples about the trouble they would soon face:

> A time is coming, and has come, when you will be scattered, each to his own home. You will leave me all alone. Yet I am not alone, for my Father is with me.
> I have told you these things, so that in me you may have peace. In this world you will have trouble. But take heart! I have overcome the world.

In Acts 8:1, we see this adversity come to fruition: "On that day a great persecution broke out against the church at Jerusalem, and all except the apostles were scattered throughout Judea and Samaria." Against that background, James, the leader of the Jerusalem church, wrote a letter to be circulated and read to these disciples, "the 12 tribes scattered among the nations" (James 1:1). In the first twelve verses of that letter, James gives us the challenge of enduring the trials of life through the wisdom that only God can give.

There are several reasons we need God's wisdom in handling adversity. The first reason is that adversity can easily produce negative attitudes. James wanted to change the disciples' attitude in verse 2, "Consider it pure joy, my brothers, whenever you face trials of many kinds." Obviously, many of these displaced and persecuted believers were confused and bitter over the trials they had fallen into. Notice that James said "whenever," not "if" we would experience trials. Trials are a fact of life, but none of us are ever adequately prepared for them. James said that these external trials of life consist of "many kinds." In other words, they are unpredictable. We can't prepare for them, but we can determine our attitude toward them before they come. The second reason we need God's wisdom is because trials often cause us to question God. In verse 3, James writes, "You know that the testing of your faith develops perseverance." Each time our faith is tested, we have to ask ourselves if God is worth trusting. If we decide that He isn't, we'll trust someone or something else for solutions. If we decide that God

today's session (cont'd)

is worth trusting in the midst of our adversity, our faith is strengthened and we develop "perseverance." <u>We also need God's wisdom because trials tend to produce impatience</u>. In verse 4, James encourages us to be patient during the difficulties of life: "Perseverance must finish its work so that you may be mature and complete, not lacking anything." God is doing a work in our lives through our trials that requires patience on our part. His desire is to use our sufferings to make us more like Christ.

In verses 5–8, James shows us how to get the wisdom we need to endure the trials of life. The first thing he tells us to do is ask God for it. In verse 5, James writes, "If any of you lacks wisdom, he should ask God." This may seem rather obvious but, surprisingly, many Christians don't think that God is concerned about the struggles they face. They may think that He's a distant God or that they are not important enough to Him. In verse 5, James reminds us that we serve a God "who gives generously to all without finding fault."

According to James 1:5–8, how should we ask God for wisdom?

Not only should we ask God for wisdom, we should be ready and willing to act on it when we receive it. Our trust in God shouldn't fluctuate up and down based on our circumstances. In verses 6–8, James puts it like this: "<u>When he asks, he must believe and not doubt</u>, because he who doubts is like a wave of the sea, blown and tossed by the wind. That man should not think he will receive anything from the Lord; he is a double-minded man, unstable in all he does." When we act on God's wisdom, we move from doubt to faith. Well-known Christian author and communicator, Ron Dunn, describes his own personal experience with the promise of James 1:5:

> The last phrase in the verse, the promise itself, says, "and it will be given to him." Period. Just like that. If I asked God for wisdom, I must have it, whether I felt wise or not. Do you know what I did? I claimed the wisdom God had promised and then began making the decisions that seemed best to me. I believe I had the right to assume that, having asked God for wisdom, his wisdom was operating in me. It was scary. At the time there was no way to know if my decisions were the "right" ones. Later, though, when that particular period was past, I could look back and see that in every instance I had made the right decision. God had kept his promise in answer to my praying.[1]

As we grow in our understanding of God's _____ as a loving _____, we will have greater confidence that our requests for wisdom will be answered.

As we grow in our understanding of God's <u>nature</u> as a loving <u>father</u>, we will have greater confidence that our requests for wisdom will be answered. In Matthew 7:7–11, Jesus put it like this:

Ask and it will be given to you; seek and you will find; knock and the door will be opened to you. For everyone who asks receives; he who seeks finds; and to him who knocks, the door will be opened.

Which of you, if his son asks for bread, will give him a stone? Or if he asks for a fish, will give him a snake? If you, then, though you are evil, know how to give good gifts to your children, how much more will your Father in heaven give good gifts to those who ask him!

What two things happen to our focus when we rely on God's wisdom?

There are two things that happen when we begin to rely on God's wisdom, instead of our own limited wisdom. First, God's wisdom moves our focus from the material to the spiritual. In God's economy, material possessions are neutral. True wisdom is evidenced by a shift in our values. We begin to focus on things that matter to God, rather than to the world. In James' day, the rich were thought of as favored by God because of their many possessions, and the poor were thought of as cursed or punished by God. In James 1:9–11, James shows us that God's wisdom values the spiritual over the material: "The brother in humble circumstances ought to take pride in his high position. But the one who is rich should take pride in his low position, because he will pass away like a wild flower. For the sun rises with scorching heat and withers the plant; its blossom falls and its beauty is destroyed. In the same way, the rich man will fade away even while he goes about his business."

The second thing that will happen when we trust in God's wisdom over our own is that our focus moves from the temporary to the eternal. In verse 12, James writes: "Blessed is the man who perseveres under trial, because when he has stood the test, he will receive the crown of life that God has promised to those who love him." Godly wisdom gives us great patience in our lives by placing our hope beyond this life. A great example of this wisdom is found in the way Moses endured the temporary pain of this world. In Hebrews 11:26, we read, "He regarded disgrace for the sake of Christ as of greater value than the treasures of Egypt, because he was looking ahead to his reward." So, when you lack wisdom (and who among us doesn't?) make sure you check with your Head Coach who is eager to guide you toward the goal line of spiritual maturity one play at a time.

notes:

12

⊕

Learning from the Story (5-7 minutes)

1. Which of the following areas usually tests your faith the most?

   ☐ parenting   ☐ marriage

   ☐ work   ☐ friends

   ☐ finances   ☐ health

   ☐ school   ☐ other:_____

2. In verses 9–11, James describes the futility of depending on riches. Which of the following possessions would you have the most difficult time giving up?

   ☐ golf clubs   ☐ photographs

   ☐ refrigerator   ☐ backyard

   ☐ clothes   ☐ cell phone

   ☐ palm pilot   ☐ television/remote control

   ☐ other:_____

3. Is there a trial you are experiencing right now in which you are finding it difficult to remain in an attitude of peace, contentment, and joy?

Remain in groups of 6–8 people, in a horseshoe configuration.

In this small-group session, students will be applying the lessons of the text to their own lives through the following questions.

The students were asked (in the student book) to choose an answer for each question and explain why.

Share with the class the following thoughts on how the lessons of this text might be applied today. The answers to the student book questions (provided in the margin) are underlined unless the question requires a personal answer.

Is seeking God's wisdom a last resort or a lifestyle for you?

What are three ways you can make seeking God's wisdom a regular part of your life?

---

life change lessons (5-7 minutes)

For many believers, seeking God's wisdom has become a last resort, rather than a lifestyle. The joy in the midst of trials that James writes about is not something that depends on circumstances. This joy is a by-product of consistently connecting with Jesus Christ. As you invest in your relationship with God on a daily basis, His joy begins to permeate your life through the work of the Holy Spirit. If circumstances are robbing you of His joy, it's likely that you've begun to trust in your own wisdom for how you respond to life's ups and downs. Here are some ways you can make seeking God's wisdom a lifestyle, rather than a last resort:

1. <u>STOP TRUSTING IN THE WORLD'S WISDOM</u>. Notice that James writes, "if anyone lacks wisdom." Some people don't think they lack wisdom and are reluctant to depend on God for direction. Later in his letter, James writes that worldly wisdom is "earthly, unspiritual, of the devil" (James 3:15). In those moments where you rely on worldly wisdom, you will find, "envy and selfish ambition … disorder and every evil practice" (James 3:16). If you are seeking wisdom from ungodly sources, your first step should be to stop seeking wisdom in all the wrong places.

2. <u>START ASKING FOR WISDOM THAT COMES FROM GOD</u>. Asking for God's wisdom is not something that should be reserved only for the times that you get into trouble. Depending on God for wisdom in life should be constant, whether or not you are experiencing adversity or ease. Prayer is a good indicator of how much you depend on God. Examine your prayer life. Your faith is only as strong as the amount of time you spend with God in prayer.

3. <u>LEARN THE WISDOM THAT GOD HAS ALREADY GIVEN YOU IN THE BIBLE</u>. The first place you should check for God's wisdom is in His written Word. Often, in times of prayer, God will bring to your mind a biblical story or Scripture that pertains to your situation. Here's a practical suggestion to help you get started. For the next 31 days, read one chapter a day out of Proverbs. This will take you a month because there are 31 chapters in the Book of Proverbs. The more you know of God's Word, the more you will know of God's wisdom.

✝

Caring Time (15-20 minutes)

CARING TIME
Remain in groups of 6–8 people, in a horseshoe configuration.

Hand out the Prayer/ Praise Report to the entire group. Ask each subgroup to pray for the empty chair. Pray specifically for God to guide you to someone to bring next week to fill that chair.

After a sufficient time of prayer in subgroups, close in a corporate prayer. Say, "Next week we will talk about: 'Choosing God's Priorities.' "

Remind participants of the daily Scripture readings and reflective questions found on page 146.

Close by sharing requests and praying for one another. During this time, pray for the trial(s) that people talked about in question 3 under "Learning from the Story." In addition, pray for the concerns on the Prayer/Praise Report.

Conclude your prayer time by reading out loud together Psalm 119:65–72:

> *Do good to your servant*
>   *according to your word, O Lord.*
> *Teach me knowledge and good judgment,*
>   *for I believe in your commands.*
> *Before I was afflicted I went astray,*
>   *but now I obey your word.*
> *You are good, and what you do is good;*
>   *teach me your decrees.*
> *Though the arrogant have smeared me with lies,*
>   *I keep your precepts with all my heart.*
> *Their hearts are callous and unfeeling,*
>   *but I delight in your law.*
> *It was good for me to be afflicted*
>   *so that I might learn your decrees.*
> *The law from your mouth is more precious to me*
>   *than thousands of pieces of silver and gold.*

12

Reference Notes

Use these notes to gain further understanding
of the text as you study on your own.

JAMES 1:1
Lord and Master

James. "James" is probably the half-brother of Jesus who was known in the early church as "James the Just."

a servant. Here he identifies Jesus as the "Lord" (master), therefore the appropriate relationship of all others to Jesus is as servants (literally "slaves").

the twelve tribes. In the New Testament, this came to be associated with the Christian church. Christians saw themselves as the new Israel (Rom. 4; 9:24–26; Phil. 3:3; 1 Peter 2:9–10).

scattered. The word is, literally, *diaspora* and was used by the Jews to refer to those of their number living outside of Israel in the Gentile world. Here it probably refers to those Jewish Christians living outside Israel (see 1 Peter 1:1).

JAMES 1:2
acceptance

Consider it pure joy. The joy James is talking about is not just a feeling. It is an active acceptance of adversity.

trials of many kinds. The word "trials" has the dual sense of "adversity" (e.g., disease, persecution, tragedy) and "temptations" (e.g., lust, greed, trust in wealth).

JAMES 1:3

perseverance. Or "endurance." It is used in the sense of active overcoming, rather than passive acceptance.

JAMES 1:4
wholeness

finish its work. Perfection is not automatic—it takes time and effort.

mature and complete. What James has in mind here is wholeness of character.

lacking. The opposite of mature and complete. This is a word used of an army that has been defeated or a person who has failed to reach a certain standard.

JAMES 1:5

wisdom. This is not just abstract knowledge, but God-given insight that leads to right living.

JAMES 1:6
answered prayer

James now contrasts the readiness on God's part to give (v. 5) with the hesitation on people's part to ask (v. 6). Both here and in James 4:3, unanswered prayer is connected to the quality of the asking, not to the unwillingness of God to give.

believe. To be one in mind about God's ability to answer prayer.

JAMES 1:8

double-minded. To doubt is to be in two minds—to believe and to disbelieve.

JAMES 1:9
children of God

The brother in humble circumstances. This refers to those who are poor in a material and social sense and who are looked down on by others because they are poor.

take pride. This becomes possible when the poor see beyond immediate circumstances to their new position as children of God.

high position. In the early church, the poor gained a new sense of self-respect.

✝

JAMES 1:10
false security

rich. The peril of riches is that people come to trust in wealth as a source of security.

low position. Jewish culture considered wealth to be a sign of God's favor. Here, as elsewhere (vv. 2,9), James reverses conventional "wisdom."

JAMES 1:11
swept away

scorching heat. The hot, southeast desert wind (the sirocco) sweeps into Israel in the spring "like a blast of hot air when an oven door is opened."

fade away. Wealth gives an uncertain security, since it is apt to be swept away as abruptly as desert flowers (Isa. 40:6–8).

JAMES 1:12
purified

Blessed. Happy is the person who has withstood all the trials to the end.

stood the test. Such a person is like metal that has been purged by fire and is purified of all foreign substances.

crown of life. Crowns were worn at weddings and feasts (and so signify joy); they were also given to the winner of an athletic competition (and so signify victory); and were worn by royalty (as befits children of God the King).

notes:

12

[1] Ron Dunn, *Don't Just Stand There, Pray Something* (Nashville, TN: Thomas Nelson, 1992), 213.

Session

13

Choosing God's Priorities

Prepare for the Session

	READINGS	REFLECTIVE QUESTIONS
Monday	James 4:13–14	How much of your future plans will impact the work of God in others?
Tuesday	James 4:15	In what areas of your life do you have difficulty being submissive to God's will?
Wednesday	James 4:16	When was the last time you boasted or bragged about something you accumulated or accomplished?
Thursday	James 4:17	What good should you be doing that you are not doing?
Friday	Ephesians 5:15	What wise decisions have you made in the past week? What unwise decisions have you made in the past week? What have these decisions taught you?
Saturday	Ephesians 5:16	How well do you take advantage of the opportunities that God gives you each day to know Him and make Him known?
Sunday	Ephesians 5:22–24	How much time do you invest in getting to know the character of God?

notes:

OUR GOALS FOR THIS SESSION ARE:

⟨U⟩ **In groups of 6–8, gather people in a horseshoe configuration.**

Make sure everyone has a name tag.

Take time to share information on class parties that are coming up as well as any relevant church events.

INTRODUCE THE ICEBREAKER ACTIVITY: The students have been given instructions in their books.

After the Icebreaker say something like, "This is our last session in this study and so it is a wise use of our time to affirm each other and thank God for all He has done. In fact, using our time wisely and according to God's priorities is what we will talk about today."

Hand out the Prayer/Praise Report. A sample copy is on pages 158-159. Have people write down prayer requests and praises. Then have the prayer coordinator collect the report and make copies for use during the Caring Time.

BIBLE STUDY
- to learn how to invest our time wisely
- to examine three ways we commonly mismanage our time
- to learn the importance of making the most of each day God gives us

LIFE CHANGE
- to write a life mission statement reflecting God's priorities
- to include prayer in our planning process
- to obey what God has already led us to do

Icebreaker (10-15 minutes)

A Winning Team. Imagine that your small group has been a football team, playing the season together. A winning team requires that people play together and that they be willing to play different roles. What roles have you seen people playing in the group? Put the name of a different person from your group next to each of the following roles. Then have people share what roles they saw each other playing.

_____ **The Quarterback**—the one who got everyone else involved

_____ **The Kicker**—the one who always "kicked in" some good points

_____ **The Wide Receiver**—the one who "caught" the most truth and applied it to his or her life

_____ **The Tight End**—the person who made sure we stayed on schedule and helped us squeeze in everything we needed to do

_____ **The Inspirational Leader**—the combination player/cheerleader who lifted us up when we needed it

_____ **Team Doctor**—the one who helped the team in so many ways without getting much attention

_____ **The Offensive Tackle**—the one who was willing to "tackle" the tough issues when they had to be faced

_____ **The Reliable Passer**—the one we could rely on to "throw" us an insight when we needed it

13

LEARNING FROM THE BIBLE

JAMES 4:13–17

Have a member of the class, selected ahead of time, read the passage from James.

Bible Study (30-45 minutes)

The Scripture for this week:

¹³Now listen, you who say, "Today or tomorrow we will go to this or that city, spend a year there, carry on business and make money." ¹⁴Why, you do not even know what will happen tomorrow. What is your life? You are a mist that appears for a little while and then vanishes. ¹⁵Instead, you ought to say, "If it is the Lord's will, we will live and do this or that." ¹⁶As it is, you boast and brag. All such boasting is evil. ¹⁷Anyone, then, who knows the good he ought to do and doesn't do it, sins.

Summarize these introductory remarks. Be sure to include the underlined information, which gives the answers to the student book questions (provided in the margin).

...about today's session (5 minutes)

WORKING THE CLOCK

Some sports use a game clock, such as football and basketball, while others don't, such as baseball and golf. In the sports where a limit is placed on the time of play, time management becomes crucial to success. At the end of a football game, the quarterback, who wants to score before time runs out, often runs out-of-bounds, calls time-outs, throws incomplete passes, and calls plays without a huddle. This is all because he wants to make the most of the time remaining in the game. Working the clock is important for us as well. <u>Our ability to stay focused and make the most of the time God has given us reflects our desire to stay focused on God's purposes.</u>

Why is it important for us, as believers, to "work the clock"?

The Old Testament story of Nehemiah illustrates the importance of eliminating distractions and avoiding anything that wastes our time. Nehemiah's great passion was rebuilding the wall around Jerusalem to bring honor to God and the restoration of His people. His mission was not without distractions. Listen to Nehemiah's description of one particular distraction and how he responded:

> When word came to Sanballat, Tobiah, Geshem the Arab and the rest of our enemies that I had rebuilt the wall and not a gap was left in it—though up to that time I had not set the doors in the gates—Sanballat and Geshem sent me this message: "Come, let us meet together in one of the villages on the plain of Ono."
>
> But they were scheming to harm me; so I sent messengers to them with this reply: "I am carrying on a great project and cannot go down. Why should the work stop while I leave it and go down to you?" Four times they sent me the same message, and each time I gave them the same answer (Neh. 6:1–4).

How did Nehemiah deal with the distractions that came with his mission?

Nehemiah knew what the priority was in his life, and he did not allow anything to distract him from the task God had given him. Nehemiah was committed to using his time wisely. Do you ever find yourself mismanaging the time God has given you to accomplish a great work in your life? Maybe God hasn't called you to build walls around a city, but maybe he's called you to develop a strong marriage, raise godly children or be a witness for Christ in your workplace and neighborhood. When distractions come at us, we can learn to say what Nehemiah said, "I am carrying on a great project and cannot go down." We can all think of ways to fill our calendars and use our time. Not all of the ways are necessarily wise. In today's session, we will learn how to manage our time wisely as we study James 4:13–17.

✚

Remain in groups of 6–8 people, in a horseshoe configuration.

In this small group session, students will be responding to the following questions that will help them share their stories in terms of James' words about priorities and future plans in James 4:13–17.

Have the students explore these questions together.

Identifying with the Story (5-7 minutes)

1. Finish this sentence with one of the endings that follow. "During my lifetime, I have spent the most time and effort planning ..."

   ☐ my retirement   ☐ my career path
   ☐ vacations and weekends ☐ my wardrobe
   ☐ lunch and dinner   ☐ my dream house
   ☐ everyone else's schedules ☐ time with my kids
   ☐ how to find the right marriage partner
   ☐ other:_____

2. Who do you know who always has a plan for the future? Who do you know who never stresses out over making plans, but prefers to act on the spur of the moment? Which person do you identify with the most?

3. Which of the future plans that you held as a teenager have been fulfilled and which ones haven't? How does your answer to this question speak to the truth of Proverbs 16:9: "In his heart a man plans his course, but the Lord determines his steps"?

13

Share with your class the following information which you may modify according to your own perspectives and teaching needs. The answers to the student book questions (provided in the margin) are underlined.

How does the way we manage our time reflect our priorities?

What is unique about the resource of time?

Based on James 4:13, what was wrong with the way the businessperson planned?

today's session (15-20 minutes)

Some of you may be able to identify with the humorous reminder that sits on the desk of Dr. John Maxwell: "God put me on earth to accomplish a certain number of things. Right now I'm so far behind I know I'll never die."[1] Many of us have schedules that are filled with more activities than we can handle. All of us have the same 24 hours in a day. The difference is in the way we choose to use our time. The way we manage our time is a great indication of what our priorities in life are. Some people choose to waste their time by taking it for granted. Others choose to spend it on their own selfish pursuits. In Matthew 6:33, Jesus shows us that the wisest investment of our time is in the pursuit of God and leading others to begin a relationship with Jesus Christ. "Seek first [God's] kingdom and [God's] righteousness, and all these [essentials of life] will be given to you as well." One of the ways God equips us to carry out the work He has for us (Eph. 2:10) is by giving us the precious resource of time. Time is the only resource we can't get more of—once it's gone, it's gone. Most of us will discover that many of the poor decisions we make are the result of a misuse of our time. In today's session, we will look at three ways that our time is commonly mismanaged.

The first way we mismanage our time is in our planning. Let's look at the plans of a businessperson that James outlines for us in verse 13: "Now listen, you who say, 'Today or tomorrow we will go to this or that city, spend a year there, carry on business and make money.' " Notice that this businessperson knew when, who, where, how long, what, and how. James did not have a problem with these plans. In fact, there's nothing wrong with planning for the future. The problem was that this person forgot to include God in the planning. James immediately sought to correct their self-sufficiency in verse 15: "Instead, you ought to say, 'If it is the Lord's will, we will live and do this or that.' " Many of us are busy making plans all the time. However, we must be careful not to plan in such a way that we squeeze God's agenda out of our lives. Instead of making plans and asking God to bless them, we should ask God to help us direct our plans toward what He's blessing. James says that we should desire the things that God wants. If this is true for us, our plans will be according to His will. Proverbs 16:3 says, "Commit to the Lord whatever you do, and your plans will succeed." Have you submitted all that you are, your thoughts and actions, to the Lord? When you do so, your plans will begin to be in accord with His plans. Proverbs 16:9 says, "In his heart a man plans his course, but the Lord determines his steps." As we include God in our planning, we should always be open to God rearranging our plans for His purposes.

The second way we mismanage our time is by presuming. We presume about our time by thinking that we will always have more time tomorrow or the next day. James responds in verse 14: "Why, you do not even know what will happen tomorrow. What is your life? You are a mist that appears for a little while and then vanishes." James is telling us that we are only fooling ourselves by making assumptions about tomorrow. Time is deceptively fleeting. We may think that we have years in the rest of our lives but we aren't promised that. Life is unpredictable and brief and leaves no room for arrogance: "As it is, you boast and brag. All such boasting is evil" (v. 16). These businesspeople presumed that their future plans were a done deal. James wanted them to know that their attitude was not from God. Proverbs 27:1 says, "Do not boast about tomorrow, for you do not know what a day may bring forth." The point is that we shouldn't plan our own futures. We should plan for the future with God involved in the process. James emphasizes that we should make the most of each day as it comes and not make plans based on assumptions about the future. In Matthew 6:34, Jesus shows us the proper attitude: "Do not worry about tomorrow, for tomorrow will worry about itself. Each day has enough trouble of its own."

According to James 4:14, what was wrong with the attitude of the businessperson?

The third way we mismanage our time is by procrastinating. This is when we put off doing the good we know God is leading us to do right now. In verse 17, James says, "Anyone, then, who knows the good he ought to do and doesn't do it, sins." The problem for many of us is that we love to put things off. "One day I'll clean out the basement." "One day I'm going to go back to school." "I'm going to start tithing, giving God at least a tenth of all my income when I have enough money." "I'll invite Bob to church next Sunday." "I'm going to start exercising when my schedule clears up." We can commit sin by doing something we shouldn't or we can commit sin by not doing something we should. Proverbs 3:27–28 gives us an example of the sin of omission: "Do not withhold good from those who deserve it, when it is in your power to act. Do not say to your neighbor, 'Come back later; I'll give it tomorrow'—when you now have it with you." Procrastination is a poor way to manage our time. Someone once said, "Delayed obedience is disobedience." When God leads us to do something, we shouldn't delay.

What was the time management problem in James 4:17?

Finish this sentence: "Delayed obedience is _____."

In Ephesians 5:15–16, the apostle Paul confirms what James is saying about being wise when we make the most of the time God has given us: "Be very careful, then, how you live—not as unwise but as wise, making the most of every opportunity, because the days are evil." In some versions, the phrase "redeeming the time" is used. The word for *redeeming* comes from the marketplace, meaning "buying up every chance or opportunity available to us." Paul wants us to "buy up" or "purchase" all the time we can before it's all gone. Have you ever gone early to a sale at a department store because you didn't want all the good deals to be gone? That's the idea Paul is conveying. Before your precious commodity of time is all gone, "buy it up" and use it for God's glory.

According to Ephesians 5:15–16, what should we do with our time?

✝

Learning from the Story (5-7 minutes)

1. Which of the plans mentioned in James 4:13 do you tend to leave God out of the most?

   ☐ planning my calendar—"today or tomorrow"
   ☐ picking the places I go—"we will go to this or that city"
   ☐ planning my future—"spend a year there"
   ☐ pursuits in life—"carrying on business"
   ☐ personal finances—"make money"

2. James says that our lives are like a "mist that appears for a little while and then vanishes" (v. 14). What kind of legacy do you want to leave behind when your time on earth is completed?

3. Can you think of a good deed you keep putting off? If so, how can this group help you do what God is leading you to do?

   ☐ Pray that God would give me the courage I'm lacking.
   ☐ Hold me accountable by asking me about it the next time you see me.
   ☐ Give me a reassurance that it is the right thing to do.
   ☐ Share a similar situation from your life and describe how you handled it.
   ☐ Other:_____

notes:

life change lessons (5-7 minutes)

It's one thing to have good intentions regarding our time, but it's quite another to prioritize our schedules to reflect God's values. Jesus knew what it meant to balance His priorities with other, less important things, that could fill His calendar. Luke 4:42–44 says, "At daybreak Jesus went out to a solitary place. The people were looking for him and when they came to where he was, they tried to keep him from leaving them. But he said, 'I must preach the good news of the kingdom of God to the other towns also, because that is why I was sent.' And he kept on preaching in the synagogues of Judea." Jesus could have filled His calendar with many good things but He chose to manage His time wisely by investing in the most important things. Here are some practical ways to help you use your time wisely:

Remain in groups of 6–8 people, in a horseshoe configuration.

In this small-group session, students will be applying the lessons of the text to their own lives through the following questions.

The students were asked (in the student book) to choose an answer for each question and explain why.

Share with the class the following thoughts on how the lessons of this text might be applied today. The answers to the student book questions (provided in the margin) are underlined unless the question requires a personal answer.

How did Jesus prioritize His schedule in Luke 4:42–44?

What three ways did the leader give you for using your time wisely?

1. <u>WRITE A LIFE MISSION STATEMENT REFLECTING GOD'S PRIORITIES</u>. If you're having trouble managing your time effectively, form a personal life mission statement and place it where you can see it every day. Begin by thinking about how you want to be remembered by your spouse, children, other family members, church members, neighbors, work associates, friends, etc. at your funeral. Write out brief statements of what you would want these individuals to share about you. Then, take the qualities from these statements and include them in a statement that begins, "My mission in life is to … ." Putting your priorities in writing will help you stay focused on what's important.

2. <u>INCLUDE PRAYER IN YOUR PLANNING PROCESS</u>. Planning is not a bad thing by itself. It's only when we leave God out of our plans or the planning process that we are treading on thin ice. Any plans worth following will be aligned with God's purposes. As we pray, we should ask God to help us do what He will bless instead of asking Him to bless what we're doing. We need to keep open the possibility that what we're planning may be out of God's will for our lives. God wants to guide our plans because He wants the best for us.

3. <u>OBEY WHAT GOD HAS ALREADY LED YOU TO DO</u>. Someone said it's not that we don't know what to do, it's that we don't want to do it. Procrastination started early for some of us when we began putting off household chores and doing our homework. In high school and college, it was manifested in late-night cramming and finishing term papers at the last minute. Putting off doing good is something we all deal with at some point. Maybe you need to ask someone for forgiveness whom you offended years ago. Maybe you owe someone money and haven't paid them back. It could be that God has wanted you to share Christ with someone but you've never found the time. Whatever the thing is, don't put it off any longer. If you're fearful, trust God to take care of the results, knowing that He has your best in mind.

notes:

13

CARING TIME
Remain in groups of 6–8 people, in a horseshoe configuration.

Hand out the Prayer/Praise Report to the group. Be sure to allow enough time for the evaluation. If your group is going to continue, also allow time to discuss the covenant on page 156. Close with a corporate prayer.

Caring Time (15-20 minutes)

Pray for the concerns listed on the Prayer/Praise Report, then continue with the evaluation and covenant.

1. Take some time to evaluate the life of your group by using the statements below. Read the first sentence out loud and ask everyone to explain where they would put a dot between the two extremes. When you are finished, go back and give your group an overall grade in the categories of Group Building, Bible Study, and Mission.

 GROUP BUILDING

On celebrating life and having fun together, we were more like a ...
wet blanket · hot tub

On becoming a caring community, we were more like a ...
prickly porcupine · · · · · · · · · · · · · · · · · · · cuddly teddy bear

 BIBLE STUDY

On sharing our spiritual stories, we were more like a ...
shallow pond · spring-fed lake

On digging into Scripture, we were more like a ...
slow-moving snail · · · · · · · · · · · · · · · · · · · voracious anteater

 MISSION

On inviting new people into our group, we were more like a ...
barbed-wire fence · wide-open door

On stretching our vision for mission, we were more like an ...
ostrich · eagle

2. What are some specific areas in which you have grown in this course?

☐ pursing God's values, rather than the values of the world
☐ putting on the full armor of God
☐ making God the delight of my life
☐ surrendering my life to the will of God
☐ accepting God's forgiveness for my sins
☐ investing in a daily time with God
☐ keeping a journal when reading and studying the Bible
☐ following the Holy Spirit's guidance
☐ seeking godly counsel
☐ trusting in God's wisdom, rather than worldly wisdom
☐ other:_____

A covenant is a promise made to another in the presence of God. Its purpose is to indicate your intention to make yourselves available to one another for the fulfillment of the purposes you share in common. If your group is going to continue, in a spirit of prayer work your way through the following sentences, trying to reach an agreement on each statement pertaining to your ongoing life together. Write out your covenant like a contract, stating your purpose, goals, and the ground rules for your group.

1. The purpose of our group will be:

2. Our goals will be:

3. We will meet on _____ (day of week).

4. We will meet for ____weeks, after which we will decide if we wish to continue as a group.

5. We will meet from _____ to _____ and we will strive to start on time and end on time.

6. We will meet at _____ (place) or we will rotate from house to house.

Caring Time (cont'd)

7. We will agree to the following ground rules for our group (check):

   ☐ **PRIORITY:** While you are in this course of study, you give the group meetings priority.

   ☐ **PARTICIPATION:** Everyone is encouraged to participate and no one dominates.

   ☐ **RESPECT:** Everyone has the right to his or her own opinion, and all questions are encouraged and respected.

   ☐ **CONFIDENTIALITY:** Anything said in the meeting is never repeated outside the meeting.

   ☐ **LIFE CHANGE:** We will regularly assess our own life change goals and encourage one another in our pursuit of Christlikeness.

   ☐ **EMPTY CHAIR:** The group stays open to reaching new people at every meeting.

   ☐ **CARE and SUPPORT:** Permission is given to call upon each other at any time especially in times of crisis. The group will provide care for every member.

   ☐ **ACCOUNTABILITY:** We agree to let the members of the group hold us accountable to the commitments which each of us make in whatever loving ways we decide upon.

   ☐ **MISSION:** We will do everything in our power to start a new group.

   ☐ **MINISTRY:** The group will encourage one another to volunteer and serve in a ministry, and to support missions by giving financially and/or personally serving.

notes:

BIBLE STUDY NOTES

Reference Notes

Use these notes to gain further understanding
of the text as you study on your own.

JAMES 4:13
the future

Boasting about the future is arrogant because God is the only one who knows what will happen in the future.

Today or tomorrow we will go. In trade, a person in the first century had to plan ahead. Travel plans, market projections, time frames, and profit forecasts are the stuff of business in all ages. Every honest merchant would plan in exactly the same way—pagan, Jew, or Christian—and that is exactly the problem James has with these plans: There is absolutely nothing about their desires for the future, their use of money, or their way of doing business that is any different from the rest of the world.

carry on business. The word James uses here is from the Greek word *emporos*, from which the English word "emporium" comes. It denotes wholesale merchants who traveled from city to city, buying and selling.

JAMES 4:14
the unknown

tomorrow. All such planning presupposes that tomorrow will unfold like any other day, when, in fact, the future is anything but secure (see Prov. 27:1).

What is your life? Is not death the great unknown? Who can know when death will come? By thinking on the worldly plane, the Christian business people James addressed have gained a false sense of security. They need to look death in the face and realize their lack of control over life.

mist. Hosea 13:3 says, "Therefore they will be like the morning mist, like the early dew that disappears, like chaff swirling from a threshing floor, like smoke escaping through a window."

JAMES 4:15
dependency on God

If it is the Lord's will. The uncertainty of the future ought not to be a terror to the Christian. Instead, it ought to force an awareness of how dependent a person is upon God, and thus move that person to a planning structure that involves God.

we will live and do this or that. James is not ruling out planning. He says plan, but keep God in mind.

JAMES 4:16
empty claims

boast. The problem with this boasting is that they are claiming to have the future under control when, in fact, it is God who holds time in His hands.

brag. This word originally described an itinerant quack who touted "cures" that did not work. It came to mean claiming to be able to do something that you could not do.

notes:

[1] Raymond McHenry, ed., *The Best of In Other Words* (Houston, TX: Raymond McHenry, 1996), 178.

Name	Phone No.